T0149716

Freedom, Love, and Action

FREEDOM, LOVE, AND ACTION

J. Krishnamurti

SHAMBHALA
Boston & London
2001

Shambhala Publications, Inc.
Horticultural Hall
300 Massachusetts Avenue
Boston, Massachusetts 02115
www.shambhala.com

For information in USA, write:
Krishnamurti Foundation of America
P.O. Box 1560
Ojai, CA 93024

Printed in the United States of America

For more information, visit www.shambhala.com.
Distributed in the United States by Random House, Inc.,
and in Canada by Random House of Canada Ltd

The Library of Congress catalogues a previous edition
of this book as follows:

Krishnamurti, J. (Jiddu), 1895–
Freedom, love, and action/J. Krishnamurti.
—1st ed. p. cm.—(Shambhala pocket classics)
Collection of five booklets based on talks given
at Brockwood Park School, England.
Contents: Five conversations—Eight conversations—
Meditations—Inward flowering—A dialogue with oneself.
ISBN 978-0-87773-977-7 (pbk.: alk. paper)
ISBN 978-1-57062-826-9
1. Conduct of life. I. Title. II. Series
B5134.K751   1994b   93-34722
181'.4—dc20   CIP

Contents

Five Conversations
1

Eight Conversations
31

Meditations 1969
75

Inward Flowering
99

A Dialogue with Oneself
123

FIVE
CONVERSATIONS

1

MEDITATION IS THE WAY of total transformation of man's mania. Man is caught in principles and ideologies which prevent him from putting an end to the conflict between himself and another. The ideology of nationality and religion and the obstinacy of his own vanity is destroying man. This destructive process goes on throughout the world. Man has tried to end it through tolerance, conciliation, through the exchange of words, and face-saving devices—but he remains entrenched in his own conditioning.

Goodness does not lie in dogma, nor in the vanity of principle and formula. These deny love, and meditation is the flowering of love.

The valley was very still that early morning. Even the owl had stopped calling his mate; his deep hoot had ceased an hour earlier. The sun wasn't up yet and the stars were still brilliant. One star was just setting over the western hills and the light from the east was slowly spreading. As the sun rose, the rocks, with dew on them, were shining, and the cactus and the leaves became silver, highly polished. And the beauty of the land began to awaken.

The monkeys were on the veranda now, two of them, red-faced, with brown coats, and tails not too long. One was scratching the other looking for insects, and when he found them he picked them out carefully and swallowed them. They were restless, and they jumped off the veranda on to the branch of a large rain tree and wandered off into the gully.

Even though the village had awakened there was still the stillness of the night. It was a peculiar stillness. It was not the absence of noise. It was not that the mind brought about the stillness or conceived it out of its own endless chattering. It was a stillness that came without asking, without any cause. And the hills, the trees, the people, the monkeys, the crows which were calling, were all in it. And it would go on until the evening. Only man was not aware of it. It would be there again when the night came, and the rocks would know it, and the newly planted banyan tree, and the lizard between the rocks.

There were four or five people in the room. Some were students, others college graduates with jobs. One of the students said, "I listened to you last year, and again this year. I know we are all conditioned. I am aware of society's brutalities, and of my own envy and anger. I know also the history of the church and its wars and its unprincipled activities. I have studied history and the endless wars of the entrenched beliefs and ideologies which are creating so much conflict in the world. This mania of mankind—which is me also—seems to hold us and we seem to be doomed forever, unless, of course, we can bring about a change in ourselves. It's the small minority that really

4

matters, that really having changed itself can do something in this murderous world. And a few of us have come,
representing others, to discuss this matter with you. I
think some of us are serious, and I don't know how far this
seriousness will carry us. So, first of all, taking us as we are,
half-serious, somewhat hysterical, unreasonable, carried
away by our assumptions and vanities—taking us as we are,
can we really change? If not, we're going to destroy each
other; our own species will disappear. There may be a rec-
onciliation in all this terror but there is always the danger
of some maniacal group letting loose the atom bomb, and
then we shall all be engulfed in it. So seeing all this, which
is fairly obvious, which is being described endlessly by au-
thors, professors, sociologists, politicians, and so on—is it
possible to change radically?"

Some of us are not quite sure that we want to change,
for we enjoy this violence. For some of us it is even profit-
able. And for others, all they desire is to remain in their
entrenched positions. There are still others who through
change seek some form of super excitement, overrated
emotional expression. Most of us want power in some form
or another—the power over oneself, the power over another, the power which comes with new and brilliant
ideas, the power of leadership, fame, and so on. Political
power is as evil as religious power. The power of the world
and the power of an ideology do not change man. Nor
does the volition to change, the will to transform oneself,
bring about this change.

"I can understand that," said the student. "Then what
is the way of change if will, if principles and ideologies are

5

not the way? Then what is the motive power? And change to what?"

The older people in the room listened to this rather seriously. They were all attentive, and not one of them looked out of the window to see the green-yellow bird sitting on a branch sunning himself that early morning, preening himself, grooming his feathers, and looking at the world from the height of that tall tree.

One of the older men said, "I am not at all sure that I want any change at all. It might be for the worse. It's better, this orderly disorder, than an order which may mean uncertainty, total insecurity, and chaos. So when you talk of how to change, and the necessity of change, I am not at all sure I agree with you, my friend. As a speculative idea I enjoy it. But a revolution which will deprive me of my job, my house, my family, and so on, is a most unpleasant idea and I don't think I want it. You're young and you can play with these ideas. All the same, I will listen and see what the outcome of this discussion will be."

The students looked at him with that superiority of freedom, with that sense of not being committed to a family, to a group, or to a political or religious party. They had said they were neither capitalist nor communist; they were not concerned with political activity at all. They smiled with tolerance and a certain feeling of awkwardness. There is that gap which exists between the older and the younger generations, and they were not going to try to bridge it.

"We are the uncommitted," the student went on, "and therefore we are not hypocrites. Of course we don't know what we want to do, but we know what is not right. We don't want social, racial differences, we're not concerned with all these silly religious beliefs and superstitions, nor do we want political leaders—though there must be a totally different kind of politics which will prevent wars. So we are really concerned, and we want to be involved in the possibilities of man's total transformation. So, to put the question again: firstly, what is this thing that is going to make us change? And secondly—change to what?"

Surely, the second question is involved in the first, isn't it? If you already know what you are changing to, is that change at all? If one knows what one will be tomorrow, then "what will be" is already in the present. The future is the present; the known future is the known present. The future is the projection, modified, of what is known now.

"Yes, I see that very clearly. So there is only, then, the question of change, not the verbal definition of what we change to. So we'll limit ourselves to the first question. How do we change? What is the drive, the motive, the force that will make us break down all barriers?"

Only complete inaction, only the complete negation of "what is." We do not see the great force that is in negation. If you reject the whole structure of principle and formula, and hence the power derived from it, the authority, that very rejection gives you the force necessary to reject all other structures of thought—and so you have the energy to change! The rejection is that energy.

"Is this what you call dying to the historical accumulation which is the present?"

7

Yes. That very dying is to be born anew. There you have the whole movement of change—the dying to the known.

"Is this rejection a positive, definite act?"

When the students revolt it is a positive, definite act, but such action is only very partial and fragmentary. It is not a total rejection. You ask, "Is it a positive act, this dying, this rejection?" It is and it isn't. When you positively leave a house and enter into another house your positive action ceases to be positive action at all because you have abandoned one power structure for another, which you will again have to leave. So this constant repetition, which appears to be a positive action, is really inaction. But if you reject the desire and the search for all inward security, then it is a total negation which is a most positive action. It is this action only which transforms man. If you reject hate and envy, in every form, you are rejecting the whole structure of what man has created in himself and outside himself. It is very simple. One problem is related to every other problem.

"So, is this what you call 'seeing the problem'?"

This seeing reveals the whole structure and nature of the problem. The seeing is not the analyzing of the problem; it is not the revealing of the cause and the effect. It is all there, laid out, as it were, on a map. It is there for you to see, and you can see it only if you have no stand from which to look, and this is our difficulty. We are committed, and inwardly it gives us great pleasure to belong. When we belong, then it is not possible to see; when we belong, we become irrational, violent, and then we want to end violence by belonging to something else. And so

8

we are caught in a vicious circle. And this is what man has done for millions of years and he vaguely calls this "evolution." Love is not at the end of time. Either it is now, or it isn't. And hell is when it is not, and the reformation of hell is the decoration of the same hell.

2

IN EUROPE spring was slipping into summer. It began in the warm south with mimosa, and then came the flowering fruit trees and the lilac, and the blue sky deepened; and you followed it north where spring was late. The chestnuts were just putting out their leaves and there were no blossoms on them yet. And the lilac was still in bud. And as you watched, the chestnut leaves became bigger, thicker, and covered the road and the view across the meadow. They were now in full bloom along the avenues in the woods, and the lilac, which had already faded in the south, was in bloom. There was a white lilac in a little yard; there were few leaves, but the white bloom seemed to cover the horizon. And as you went up north, spring was just beginning. The tulips, whole fields of them, were in bloom, and the ducks had their yellow little chicks who paddled rapidly after the mother in the still water of the canal. The lilac was still in bloom and the trees were still bare, and as the days went by, spring was ripening. And the flat earth, with its vast horizon and clouds so low you felt you could touch them, stretched from side to side.

Spring was in full glory here; there was no separateness. The tree and you and those ducks with their little chicks, the tulips and the vast expanse of the sky—there was no separation. The intensity of it made the color of the tulip, the lily, and the tender green leaf, so vivid, so close, that the senses were the flowers, the man and the woman who went by on their bicycles, and the crow high up in the air. There is really no separateness between the new grass, the child, and yourself: we do not know how to look, and the looking is the meditation.

He was a young man, bright, clear-eyed, and urgent. He said he was thirty-five or so, and had a good job. He was not bothered by nationalism, racial disturbances, or the conflicts of religious beliefs. He said he had a problem and hoped he could discuss it without being vulgar, without slipping into crude expressions. He said he was married and had a child, and the child was lovely, and he hoped she would grow up into a different world. His problem was, he said, sex. It was not the adjustment to his wife, nor was there another woman in his life. He said it was becoming a problem because he seemed to be consumed by it. His job, which he did fairly well, was wrapped up with his sexual thoughts. He wanted more and more of it—the pleasure and the enjoyment, the beauty and the tenderness of it. He didn't want to make it into a problem, as it was with most people who were either frigid or made the whole of life a sexual issue. He loved his wife and he felt he was beginning to use her for his own personal pleasure; and now his appetite was growing and not lessening with the years, and it was becoming a great burden.

11

Before we go into this problem, I think we should understand what love and chastity are. The vow of chastity is not chastity at all, for below the words the craving goes on, and trying to suppress it in different ways, religious and otherwise, is a form of ugliness which, in its very essence, is unchaste. The chastity of the monk, with his vows and denials, is essentially worldliness, which is unchaste. All forms of resistance build a wall of separateness which turns life into a battlefield; and so life becomes not chaste at all. Therefore one has to understand the nature of resistance. Why do we resist at all? Is it the outcome of traditional fear—fear of going wrong, of stepping out of line?

Society has imprinted its respectability so deeply on us that we want to conform. If we had no resistance at all, would we become unbalanced? Would our appetites increase? Or is this very resistance breeding the conflict and the neurosis?

To walk through life without resistance is to be free, and freedom, whatever it does, will always be chaste. The word *chastity* and the word *sex* are brutal words; they do not represent reality. Words are false, and love is not a word. When love is pleasure, there is pain and fear in it, and so love goes out of the window, and life becomes a problem. Why is it that we have made sex into such an enormous issue—not only in our personal lives but also in the magazines, the films, the pictures, the religions which have condemned it? Why has man given such extraordinary importance to this fact of life, and not to the other facts of life, like power and cruelty?

To deny sex is another form of brutality; it is there, it is

12

a fact. When we are intellectual slaves, endlessly repeating what others have said, when we are following, obeying, imitating, then a whole avenue of life is closed; when action is merely a mechanical repetition and not a free movement, then there is no release; when there is this incessant urge to fulfill, to be, then we are emotionally thwarted, there is a blockage. So sex becomes the one issue which is our very own, which is not secondhand. And in the act of sex there is a forgetting of oneself, one's problems and one's fears. In that act there is no self at all. This self-forgetfulness is not only in sex, but comes also with drink, or drugs, or in watching some game. It is this self-forgetfulness that we are seeking, identifying ourselves with certain acts or with certain ideologies and images, and so sex becomes a problem. Then chastity becomes a thing of great importance, or the enjoyment of sex, the chewing over it, the endless images, become equally important.

When we see this whole thing, what we make of love, of sex, of self-indulgence, of taking vows against it—when we see this whole picture, not as an idea but as an actual fact, then love, sex, and chastity are one. They are not separate. It is the separation in relationship that corrupts. Sex can be as chaste as the blue sky without a cloud; but the cloud comes and darkens, with thought. Thought says, "This is chaste, and this is indulgence," "This must be controlled," and "In this I will let myself go." So thought is the poison, not love, not chastity, not sex.

That which is innocent, whatever it does, is always chaste; but innocence is not the product of thought.

3

"WHAT IS ACTION?" he asked. "And what is love? Is there a link between them, or are they two different things?"

He was a big man and had long hair, almost touching his shoulders, which emphasized the squareness of his face. He wore corduroy trousers and had an air of roughness. He was soft-spoken, with a ready smile and a quick mind. He wasn't particularly interested in himself but was keen to ask questions and to find the right answers.

Love and action are not separate; they are made separate by thought. Where there is love, action is part of it. Action by itself has very little meaning. Action is the response to challenge, and the response is from the background of culture, social influences, and tradition, so it is always old. Challenge is always new, otherwise you wouldn't call it challenge. Unless response is adequate to challenge there must be conflict, and therefore decay. Our actions, springing from the past, must ever lead to disorder and decay.

"So, is there an action which is not in itself the cause

of decay? And is such action possible in this world?" he asked.

It is possible only when we understand the nature of challenge. Is there only one challenge, or are there multiple challenges? Or, do we translate this one challenge into diversified and fragmentary challenges? Surely there is only one, but our mind, being fragmentary, translates that one challenge into many and tries to respond to these multiple fragments. And so our actions become contradictory and conflicting, causing misery and confusion in all our relationships.

"That I see," he said, "our minds are fragmentary; I see that very clearly, but what is this one challenge?"

It is that man should be completely, totally, free. Not free from any one particular issue or from one particular bondage, but from all bondages and from all issues. When you accept the challenge—and this challenge has always been there for man to accept from the most ancient of times until now—you cannot possibly interpret it according to any condition of culture or society. To deny freedom is to retrogress. Can you accept this challenge, not intellectually, but with the impact, with the intensity, of some acute and dangerous disease? If you do not accept it, then you are merely acting according to your own personal pleasure and idiosyncrasy, which make for bondage, slavery to a particular pattern of thought. If you do not accept this challenge—that man be completely free—then you deny love. Then action is a series of adjustments to social and environmental demands, with agonies, despairs, and fears.

"But can one be so completely free, living in this murderous world?"

That is a wrong question. That is merely an intellectual
inquiry which has very little validity. Be free, and then
you will love, in whatever society or culture. Without freedom man withers away, however great his work, whether
in art, science, politics, or religion. Freedom and action
are not separate. Being free is action; it isn't that there is
action to be free, doing in order to be free. Love, and hate
ceases. But to deny hate in order to love is part of that
pleasure which thought establishes. So freedom, love, and
action are interrelated, not to be separated, not to be cut
up into political or social activity, and so on. The mind,
being established in freedom, acts. And this action is love.

4

WE WENT PAST the well-known village which had become fashionable both in winter and in summer, along a stream; and the car turned to the right and went through a valley with steep hills on both sides covered with pine trees. Occasionally, high up in the openings in the pine trees, we saw the chamois playing about. The road went along the stream, and then we climbed, not too steeply. One could have walked up the slope very easily. We entered an unpaved road which was very dusty and rough, with big potholes, and another lovely stream full of green-blue water was by its side. The car couldn't go any further and the path went on through a thin pine wood where many of the trees had been uprooted by the recent storm. This path through the silent wood became more and more quiet and lonely. There were no birds here, there was only the song of the water as it rushed down over the rocks and fallen trees, over the big boulders. That was the only sound; and here and there the water was very quiet, in deep pools where one could have bathed if the water hadn't been too cold. Here there were many wild flowers,

17

yellow, violet, and pink. It was really a beautiful place, full of the sound of the river, cascading down. But over it all there was that strange silence that exists where man has not been. There was moss underfoot; a leaning tree was covered with it, and in the sunlight it was very brilliant green and yellow. On the other side of the ravine one could see the evening light of the sun and the brilliant green of a meadow that stretched upward to the sky, which was intensely blue.

The silence enveloped you, and you remained there quietly, watching the light, listening to the water and to the intense silence which no breeze disturbed. It was a lovely evening, and it seemed a pity to return.

He was a youngish man and had probably studied human nature a little, not only from books but from observation, from talking to many people. He had traveled extensively and said that he had met many people and was interested in this whole business of man's relationship to himself. He had witnessed the recent students' riots in different parts of the world, this spontaneous outburst against the established order, and apparently he knew some of the leaders, both in the south and in the north. He was concerned with the uncovering of the self that is hidden both in the subconscious as well as in the upper layers of consciousness.

He said, "I see the necessity of exploring this whole field and dying to it, so that a new thing can come into being, but I can't die to something I don't know—the subconscious, the deeper layers which lie so secretly hidden, which are a fathomless storehouse of things unknown or half-forgotten, which respond and contract from a source which remains covered. Though you have said the subconscious is as trivial as the conscious, and that therefore it is of very little importance, though you have compared it to a computer and have pointed out that it is mechanical, yet this subconscious is responsible for all our behavior, all our relationships. How can you call it trivial? Do you realize what you are saying?"

To understand all this, which is quite a complex problem, it is important to look at the whole structure of consciousness and not break it up into the conscious and the hidden. We accept this division as natural, but is it natural, or is it an observation from a fragment? Our difficulty is going to be to see the whole and not the fragment. Then the problem arises as to who is the observer who sees the whole. Is he not also a fragment who can therefore only look fragmentarily?

"Are we ever the whole, or only fragments acting separately in contradiction?"

We must be clear on this question of the whole and the fragment. Can we ever see the whole, or have a feeling of the whole, through this fragment? Do you see the whole tree or only a branch of the tree? You can see the whole of the tree if you are at a certain distance—not too far and yet not too close. If you are too close, you see only the various separate branches. So to see the whole of anything there must be—not the space that the word creates—but the space of freedom. Only in freedom can you see the whole. We are, as you said, sir, always acting in fragments

19

which are in opposition to each other, or in a fragment which is in harmony with one other fragment.

"Our whole life is broken up into the family, the businessman, the citizen, the artist, the sensualist, the good man, and so on. We know only this fragmentary action with its terrible tensions and delights."

These fragments have their own hidden motives opposed to other hidden motives which are different and contradictory, and the upper layers of consciousness respond according to these underground opposing elements of conditioning. So we are a bundle of contradictory motives and drives which respond to environmental challenge.

"The everyday mind is these responses in actual action, and in conflict which is actually visible."

So then what is the problem? What do you want to resolve or understand?

"The problem is that I must see the totality of all these hidden motives and conditionings which are responsible for the visible conflict. In other words, I must see the so-called subconscious. Even if I were not in conflict—and I am in conflict—even if I weren't, then I'd still have to know all this subconscious in order to know myself at all. And can I ever know myself?"

Either you know what has happened or what is actually taking place. To know what is actually taking place you are looking with the eyes of the past, and therefore you don't know what is happening. Looking with the eyes of the past at the living present means not seeing it. So the word *know* is a dangerous word, as all words are dangerous and false. When you say, "I want to know myself," there are two things involved. Who is the entity who says, "I must know myself," and what is there, apart from himself, to know? And so it becomes an absurd question! So the observer is the observed. The observer is the entity who dreams, who is in conflict, who wants to know and wants to be known, the illusion and the demand to end the illusion, the dream which he interprets on waking and the interpretation which depends on conditioning. He is the whole, the analyzed and the analyzer, the experiencer and the experience. He is the whole. He is the maker of god and its worshipper. All this is a fact which actually is, which anybody with a little observation can see. Then, what is the question? The question is this, isn't it, sir: Is there any action within this framework which will not create more conflict, more misery, more confusion, more chaos? Or is there an action outside this historical accumulation?

"Are you asking if there is a part of me which can operate on this accumulation, which is not of it?"

You mean, am I positing some Atman, soul, divinity within you which is untouched?

"It looks like it."

Certainly not, sir. Nothing of the kind. When you put this question you are really repeating an old tradition of escape. We have to think this out anew, not repeat a timeworn superstition. Within this framework of the "me," the ego, the self, obviously there is no freedom, and therefore it is always breeding its own misery—social, personal, and so on. Is it ever possible to be free from this? We spend our energies discussing political, religious, social freedom, freedom from poverty and inequality, and so on.

"I agree with you, sir. We spend our time asking if we can be free to act, to change the social structure, to break down social disorder, poverty, inequality, and so on, and I am not at all sure we want freedom at all."

Does freedom lie within the structure of this accumulated past, or outside the structure? Freedom is necessary, and freedom cannot be within this structure. So you are asking, really, is it possible for man to go beyond this structure, to be free—that is, to act not from this structure? To be, to act, and to live outside this framework? There is such a freedom and it comes into being only when there is the total denial of—not resistance to—what actually is, without having a secret longing for freedom. So the negation of what is, is freedom.

"How do you deny it?"

You can't deny it! If you say, "I will deny it," you are back again within the framework. But the very seeing of what is, is the freedom from it, and this may be called "denial" or any other word you care to use. So the seeing becomes all-important, not all this rigmarole of words, cunning subtleties, and devious explanations. The word is not the thing, but we are concerned with the word and not with the seeing.

"But we are right back where we started! How can I see the totality of myself, and who is there to see it, since the observer is the observed?"

As we said previously, sir, you can't see. There is only

seeing, not "you" seeing. The "what is" is before your eyes. This is seeing, this is the truth.

"Is it important to see the structure which operates, or the content of that structure?"

What is important is to see the whole, not as structure and content, but to see that the structure is the content and the content is the structure, the one cannot exist without the other. So what is important is to see.

5

THOUGHT can never penetrate very deeply into any problem of human relationship. Thought is superficial and old and is the outcome of the past. The past cannot enter into something that is totally new. It can explain the new, organize it, communicate it, but the word is not the new. Thought is the word, the symbol, the image. Without this symbol is there thought? We have used thought to reconstruct, to change the social structure. Thought, being old, reforms that structure into a new pattern based upon the old. And basically, thought is divisive, fragmentary, and whatever it does will be separative and contradictory. However much it may explain philosophically or religiously the new and necessary social structure, in it there will always be the seed of destruction, of war, and of violence. Thought is not the way to the new. Only meditation opens the door to that which is everlastingly new. Meditation is not a trick of thought. It is the seeing of the futility of thought and the ways of the intellect. Intellect and thought are necessary in the operation of anything mechanical, but the intellect is a fragmentary perception of the whole, and meditation is the seeing of the whole. Intellect can operate only in the field of the known. That is why life becomes a monotonous routine from which we try to escape through revolts and revolutions—merely to fall back once again into another field of the known. This change is no change at all as it is the product of thought which is always old. Meditation is the flight from the known. There is only one freedom: it is from the known. And beauty and love lie in this freedom.

It was a small room overlooking a lovely valley. It was early in the morning, the sun breaking through the clouds and giving light here and there to the hills, to the meadows, and to the flashing stream. Probably later it would rain, there would be wind, but now the valley was still and undisturbed. The mountains seemed very close, almost as if you could touch them, though they were far and hard to reach. They had snow upon them, and it was melting in the early summer sun. When the sun showed, the hills cast deep shadows on the valley, and the dandelions and the bright wild flowers in the field would be out. It was not a very wide valley and a stream ran through it swiftly, with the noise of the mountains. The water was clear now, a grey-blue, and as the snow melted it would become muddy and fast-moving. There was a red-coated squirrel who sat on the grass and looked at us, full of curiosity, but always on guard, ready to scurry up the tree to a higher branch. When it did, it stopped and looked down to see if we were still there. It soon lost its curiosity and went on with its own business.

The room was small, with uncomfortable chairs and a

cheap carpet on the floor. He sat on the most comfortable chair, a big man and an important man, a high bureaucrat, very high indeed. And there were others, students, the hostess, and some guests. The official sat quietly, but he was tired. He had come a long way, many hours in the air, and was glad to sit in a more or less comfortable chair.

The student said, "You people have made a terrible world of blood and tears. You have had every chance to make a different world. You are highly educated, hold an important position—and you can't do anything. You really support the established order with its brutalities, inequalities, and all the ugly mess of the present social world. We, the younger generation, despise all this, we're in revolt against it. We know that you're all hypocrites. We are not of any group or of any political or religious body. We have no race, we have no gods, for you have deprived us of what might have been a reality. You have divided the world into nationalities. We are against all this, but we don't know what we want. We don't know where we're going, but we know very well that what you offer us, we don't want. And the gap between you and us is very wide indeed; and probably it can never be bridged. We are new, and we are wary of falling into the trap of the old."

"You *will* fall into it," he said, "only it will be a new trap. You may not kill each other physically, and I hope you won't, but you'll kill each other at a different level, intellectually, with words, cynicism, and bitterness. This has been the age-old cry against the older generation, but now it is more articulate, more effective. You may call me a bourgeois, and I am. I have worked hard to bring about

26

a better world, helped to allay antagonism and opposition, but it isn't easy; when two opposing beliefs, ideologies, meet, there is bound to be hatred, war, and concentration camps. We're also against it, and we think we can do something but there really is very little we can do."

He wasn't defending himself. He was just stating simple facts as he saw them. But the student, being very bright, saw this and smiled unyieldingly.

"We're not accusing you. We have nothing to do with you; and that is the trouble. We want a different world, of love; we want matters of government decided by computers, not by personal interests and ambitions, not by power groups, religious or political. So there is this gulf. We have taken a stand, and some of us at least won't yield on this matter."

The important man must have been young once, full of zeal and brightly curious, but now it was over. What makes the mind dull? The clamorous demands of the younger generation will soon calm down when they get married, settle down, and have children and responsibilities. Their minds which were once so sharp will become dull. They, too, will become bourgeois. Perhaps a few escape from this agony—if they don't become specialized and astonishingly capable.

"I suppose," he said, "my mind has lost its elasticity, its flame, because I really have nothing to live for. I used to be religious but I've seen too many priests in high positions and they have dispelled all my hopes. I've studied hard, worked hard, and I'm trying to bring opposite elements together, but it's all part of a routine now, and I'm well aware that I'm fading away."

"Yes," said the student, "there are some of us who are very bright, sharp as needles, brilliantly articulate, but I can see the danger of their becoming successful leaders. There is the hero worship, and gradually the brilliance of youth and brightness of perception fade. I, too, have often asked myself why it is that everything becomes dull, worn out, and meaningless—sex, love, and the beauty of the morning. The artist wants to express something new, but it is still the same old mind and body behind the paintings."

This is one of the common factors of the relationship between the old and the young—the slow contagion of time and sorrow, the anxieties, and the bitter pill of self-pity. What makes the mind dull—the mind, which is so extraordinarily capable of inventing new things, of going to the moon, of building computers, of so many things that are really extraordinary, almost magical? Of course, it is the collective mind that has produced the computer or composed a sonata. The collective, the group, is a common thought which is both in the many and in the one. Therefore there is not the collective or the one—only thought. The individual fights the collective and the collective fights the individual, but what is common to both is thought. And it is thought that makes the mind dull, whether the thought be in the interests of the one or of the many, the thought of self-improvement or the social upheaval. Thought is always in search of the secure—the security that is in the house, in the family, in the belief,

28

or the security that denies all this. Thought is security, and the security is not only in the past from which the future security is built, but also the security that it tries to establish beyond time.

There was a silence. And a sparrow came onto the balcony where there were a few crumbs of bread and was pecking at them. Soon its young came too, fluttering their wings, and the mother began to feed them, one after the other. And a patch of blue sky, so intense, appeared over the green hill.

"But we can't do without thought," said the student. "All our books, everything that's written, put down on paper, is the result of thought. And do you mean to say all this is unnecessary? There would be no education at all if you had your way. Is this so? It seems rather strange and fantastic. You appeared a few moments ago quite intelligent. Are you going back into primitivism?"

Not at all. What are you educated for anyway? You may be a sociologist, an anthropologist, or a scientist, with your specialized mind working away at a fragment of the whole field of life. You are filled with knowledge and words, with capable explanations and rationalizations. And perhaps in the future the computer will be able to do all this infinitely better than you can. Education may have a different meaning altogether—not merely transferring what is printed on a page to your brain. Education may mean opening the doors of perception to the vast movement of life. It may mean learning how to live happily, freely, not with hate and confusion, but in beatitude. Modern education is blinding us; we learn to fight each other more and more, to compete, to struggle with each other. Right education is surely finding a different way of life, setting the mind free from its own conditioning. And perhaps then there can be love, which in its action will bring about true relationship between man and man.

EIGHT
CONVERSATIONS

1

QUESTIONER: I should like, suddenly, to find myself in a totally different world, supremely intelligent, happy, with a great sense of love. I'd like to *be* on the other bank of the river, not to have to struggle across, asking the experts the way. I have wandered in many different parts of the world and looked at man's endeavors in different fields of life. Nothing has attracted me except religion. I would do anything to get to the other shore, to enter into a different dimension and see everything as though for the first time with clear eyes. I feel very strongly that there must be a sudden break through from all this tawdriness of life. There must be!

Recently when I was in India I heard a temple bell ringing and it had a very strange effect on me. I suddenly felt an extraordinary sensation of unity and beauty such as I had never felt before. It happened so suddenly that I was rather dazed by it, and it was real, not a fancy or an illusion. Then a guide came along and asked me if he could show me the temples, and on that instant I was back again in the world of noise and vulgarity. I want to recapture it but of course, as you say, it is only a dead memory and therefore valueless. What can I do, or not do, to get to the other shore?

KRISHNAMURTI: There is no way to the other shore. There is no action, no behavior, no prescription that will open the door to the other. It is not an evolutionary process; it is not the end of a discipline; it cannot be bought or given or invited. If this is clear, if the mind has forgotten itself and no longer says "the other bank" or "this bank," if the mind has stopped groping and searching, if there is total emptiness and space in the mind itself, then and only then is it there.

Q: I understand what you say verbally, but I can't stop groping and longing, for deep within me I do not believe that there is no way, no discipline, no action that will bring me to the other shore.

K: What do you mean by "I do not believe there is no way"? Do you mean a teacher will take you by the hand and carry you over?

Q: No. I do hope, though, that someone who understands will directly point to it, for it must actually be there all the time since it is real.

K: Surely all this is supposition. You had that sudden feeling of reality when you heard the temple bell, but that is a memory, as you said, and from that you are drawing a conclusion that it must be there always for it is real. Reality is a peculiar thing; it is there when you are not looking, but when you do look, with greed, what you capture is the sediment of your greed, not reality. Reality is a living thing and cannot be captured, and you cannot say it is always there. There is a path only to something which is stationary, to a fixed, static point. To a living thing, which is constantly in movement, which has no resting place, how can there be a guide, a path? The mind is so eager to attain it, to grasp it, that it makes it into a dead thing. So can you put aside the memory of that state which you had? Can you put aside the teacher, the path, the end—put it aside so completely that your mind is empty of all this seeking? At present your mind is so occupied with this overwhelming demand that the very occupation becomes a barrier. You are seeking, asking, longing, to walk on the other shore. The other shore implies that there is this shore, and from this shore to get to the other shore there is space and time. That is what is holding you and bringing about this ache for the other shore. That is the real problem—time that divides, space that separates, the time necessary to get there, and the space that is the distance between this and that. This wants to become that, and finds it is not possible because of the distance and the time it takes to cover that distance. In this there is not only comparison but also measurement, and a mind that is capable of measuring is capable also of illusion. This division of space and time between this and that is the way of the mind, which is thought. Do you know, when there is love, space disappears and time disappears? It is only when

35

thought and desire come in that there is a gap of time to be bridged. When you see this, this is that.

Q: But I don't see it. I feel that what you say is true, but it eludes me.

K: Sir, you are so impatient, and that very impatience is its own aggressiveness. You are attacking, asserting. You are not quiet to look, to listen, to feel deeply. You want to get to the other shore at any cost and you are swimming frantically, not knowing where the other shore is. The other shore may be this shore, and so you are swimming away from it. If I may suggest it: stop swimming. This doesn't mean that you should become dull, vegetate, and do nothing, but rather that you should be passively aware without any choice whatsoever and no measurement. Then see what happens. Nothing may happen, but if you are expecting that bell to ring again, if you are expecting all that feeling and delight to come back, then you are swimming in the opposite direction. To be quiet requires great energy; swimming dissipates that energy. You need all your energy for silence of the mind, and it is only in emptiness, in complete emptiness, that a new thing can be.

2

QUESTIONER: All so-called religious people have something in common and I see this same thing in most of the people who come to hear you. They are all looking for something which they variously call nirvana, liberation, enlightenment, self-realization, eternity, or God. Their goal is defined and held before them in various teachings, and each of these teachings, these systems, has its set of sacred books, its disciplines, its teachers, its morality, its philosophy, its promises and threats—a straight and narrow path excluding the rest of the world and promising at its end some heaven or other. Most of these seekers move from one system to another, substituting the latest teaching for the one they have recently dropped. They move from one emotional orgy to another, not thinking that the same process is at work in all this seeking. Some of them remain in one system with one group and refuse to budge. Others eventually believe that they have realized whatever it is they wanted to realize, and then they spend their days in some withdrawn beatitude attracting in their turn a group of disciples who start the whole cycle over again.

In all this there is the compulsive greed to attain some realization and, usually, the bitter disappointment and frustration of failure. All this seems to me very unhealthy. These people sacrifice ordinary living for some imaginary goal and a most unpleasant feeling emanates from this kind of milieu: fanaticism, hysteria, violence, and stupidity. One is surprised to find among them certain good writers who otherwise seem quite sane. All this is called religion. The whole thing stinks to high heaven. This is the incense of piety. I have observed it everywhere. This search for enlightenment causes great havoc, and people are sacrificed in its wake. Now I would like to ask you, is there in fact any such thing as enlightenment and, if so, what is it?

KRISHNAMURTI: If it is an escape from everyday living—everyday living being the extraordinary movement of relationship—then this so-called realization, this so-called enlightenment, or whatever name you like to give it, is illusion and hypocrisy. Anything that denies love and the understanding of life and action is bound to create a great deal of mischief. It distorts the mind, and life is made a horrible affair. So if we take that to be axiomatic then perhaps we may proceed to find out if enlightenment— whatever that may mean—can be found in the very act of living. After all, living is more important than any idea, ideal goal, or principle. It is because we don't know what living is that we invent these visionary, unrealistic concepts which offer escape. The real question is, can one find enlightenment in living, in the everyday activities of

38

life, or is it only for the few who are endowed with some extraordinary capacity to discover this beatitude? Enlightenment means to be a light unto oneself, but a light which is not self-projected or imagined, which is not some personal idiosyncrasy. After all, this has always been the teaching of true religion, though not of organized belief and fear.

Q: You say the teaching of true religion! This immediately creates the camp of the professionals and specialists versus the rest of the world. Do you mean, then, that religion is separate from life?

K: Religion is not separate from life; on the contrary, it is life itself. It is this division between religion and life which has bred all the misery you are talking about. So we come back to the basic question of whether it is possible in daily life to live in a state which, for the moment, let us call enlightenment.

Q: I still don't know what you mean by enlightenment.

K: A state of negation. Negation is the most positive action, not positive assertion. This is a very important thing to understand. Most of us so easily accept positive dogma, a positive creed, because we want to be secure, to belong, to be attached, to depend. The positive attitude divides and brings about duality. The conflict then begins between this attitude and others. But the negation of all values, of all morality, of all beliefs, having no frontiers,

39

cannot be in opposition to anything. A positive statement in its very definition separates, and separation is resistance. To this we are accustomed, this is our conditioning. To deny all this is not immoral; on the contrary to deny all division and resistance is the highest morality. To negate everything that man has invented, to negate all his values, ethics, and gods, is to be in a state of mind in which there is no duality, therefore no resistance or conflict between opposites. In this state there are no opposites, and this state is not the opposite of something else.

Q: Then how do you know what is good and what is bad? Or is there no good and bad? What is to prevent me from crime or even murder? If I have no standards what is to prevent me from God knows what aberrations?

K: To deny all this is to deny oneself, and oneself is the conditioned entity who continually pursues a conditioned good. To most of us, negation appears as a vacuum because we know activity only in the prison of our conditioning, fear, and misery. From that we look at negation and imagine it to be some terrible state of oblivion or emptiness. To the man who has negated all the assertions of society, religion, culture, and morality, the man who is still in the prison of social conformity is a man of sorrow. Negation is the state of enlightenment which functions in all the activities of a man who is free of the past. It is the past with its tradition and its authority that has to be negated. Negation is freedom, and it is the free man who lives, loves, and knows what it means to die.

Q: That much is clear; but you say nothing about any intimation of the transcendental, the divine, or whatever you like to call it.

K: The intimation of that can be found only in freedom, and any statement about it is the denial of freedom; any statement about it becomes a verbal communication without meaning. It is there, but it cannot be found or invited, least of all imprisoned in any system, or ambushed by any clever tricks of the mind. It is not in the churches or the temples or the mosques. There is no path to it, no guru, no system that can reveal its beauty; its ecstasy comes only when there is love. This is enlightenment.

Q: Does it bring any new understanding of the nature of the universe or of consciousness or being? All the religious texts are full of that sort of thing.

K: It is like asking questions about the other shore while living and suffering on this shore. When you are on the other shore you are everything and nothing, and you never ask such questions. All such questions are of this shore and really have no meaning at all. Begin to live and you will be there without asking, without seeking, without fear.

3

QUESTIONER: I see the importance of ending fear, sorrow, anger, and all the travail of man. I see that one must lay the foundations of good behavior, which is generally called righteousness, and that in that there is no hatred or envy and none of the brutality in which man exists. I see also that there must be freedom—not from any particular thing but freedom in itself—and that one must not be always in the prison of one's own demands and desires. I see all this very clearly and I try—though perhaps you may not like the word *try*—to live in the light of this understanding. I have to some extent gone deeply into myself. I am not held by any of the things of this world, nor by any religion. Now I would like to ask: granted that one is free, not only outwardly but inwardly, of all the misery and confusion of life, what is there beyond the wall? When I say "the wall," I mean fear, sorrow, and the constant pressure of thought. What is there that can be seen when the mind is quiet, not committed to any particular activity?

KRISHNAMURTI: What do you mean when you say, "What is there?" Do you mean something to be perceived, to be felt, to be experienced, or to be understood? Are you asking, by any chance, "What is enlightenment?" Or are you asking, "What is there when the mind has stopped all its wanderings and has come to quietness?" Are you asking what there is on the other side when the mind is really still?

Q: I'm asking all these things. When the mind is still, there seems to be nothing. There must be something tremendously important to discover behind all thought. The Buddha and one or two others have talked about something so immense that they can't put it into words. The Buddha said, "Don't measure with words the immeasurable." Everyone has known moments when the mind was perfectly still, and there was really nothing so very great about it; it was just emptiness. And yet one has a feeling that there is something just around the corner which, once discovered, transforms the whole of life. It would seem, from what people have said, that a still mind is necessary to discover this. Also, I see that only an uncluttered, still mind can be efficient and truly perceptive. But there must be something much more than simply an uncluttered, still mind, something much more than a fresh mind, an innocent mind—more even than a loving mind.

K: So what is the question now? You have stated that a quiet, sensitive, alert mind is necessary, not only to be efficient, but also to perceive things around you and in yourself.

43

Q: All the philosophers and scientists are perceiving something all the time. Some of them are remarkably bright, many of them are even righteous. But when you've looked through everything they've perceived or created or expressed, it's really not very much, and there is certainly no intimation of anything divine.

K: Are you asking if there is something sacred beyond all this? Are you asking if there is a different dimension in which the mind can live and perceive something that is not merely the intellectual formulation of cunning? Are you asking in a roundabout way if there is or is not something supreme?

Q: A great many people have said in the most convincing way that there is a tremendous treasure which is the source of consciousness. They all agree that it cannot be described. They disagree about how to perceive it. They all seem to think that thought must stop before it can manifest itself. Some say it is the very matter from which thought is made, and so on, and so on. All agree that you are not really living unless you have discovered it. Apparently you yourself say more or less the same thing. Now I'm not following any system or discipline or guru or belief. I don't need any of these things to tell me there is something transcendental. When you look at a leaf or at a face, you realize that there is something far greater than the scientific or biological explanations of existence. It seems that you have drunk at this source. We listen to what you say. You carefully show the triviality and the limitation of thought. We listen, we reflect, and we do come upon a new stillness. Conflict does end. But what then?

K: Why are you asking this?

Q: You're asking a blind man why he wants to see.

K: The question wasn't asked as a clever gambit, or in order to point out that a silent mind doesn't ask anything at all, but to find out whether you are really searching for something transcendental. If you are, what is the motive behind that search—curiosity, an urgency to discover, or the desire to see such beauty as you have never seen before? Isn't it important for you to find out for yourself whether you are asking for the more, or whether you are trying to see exactly what is? The two are incompatible. If you can put aside the more, then we are concerned only with what is when the mind is silent. What actually takes place when the mind is really quiet? That is the real question, isn't it—not what is transcendental or what lies beyond?

Q: What lies beyond is my question.

K: What lies beyond can be found only if the mind is still. There may be something or there may be nothing at all. So the only thing that is important is for the mind to be still. Again, if you are concerned with what lies beyond, then you are not looking at what the state of actual stillness is. If stillness to you is only a door to that which

45

lies beyond, then you are not concerned with that door, whereas what is important is the very door itself, the very stillness itself. Therefore you cannot ask what lies beyond. The only thing that is important is for the mind to be still. Then what takes place? That is all we are concerned with, not with what lies beyond silence.

Q: You are right. The silence has no importance to me except as a doorway.

K: How do you know it is a doorway and not the thing itself? The means is the end, they are not two separate things. Silence is the only fact, not what you discover through it. Let us remain with the fact and see what that fact is. It is of great importance, perhaps of the greatest importance, that this silence be silence in itself and not something induced as a means to an end, not something induced through drugs, discipline, or the repetition of words.

Q: The silence comes of its own, without a motive and without a cause.

K: But you are using it as a means.

Q: No, I have known silence and I see that nothing happens.

K: That is the whole point. There is no other fact but silence which has not been invited, induced, sought after, but which is the natural outcome of observation and of understanding oneself and the world about one. In this there has been no motive which has brought silence. If there is any shadow or suspicion of a motive, then that silence is directed and deliberate, so it is not silence at all. If you can honestly say that that silence is free, then what actually takes place in that silence is our only concern. What is the quality and the texture of that silence? Is it superficial, passing, measurable? Are you aware of it after it is over, or during the silence? If you are aware that you have been silent, then it is only a memory, and therefore dead. If you are aware of the silence while it is happening, then is it silence? If there is no observer—that is, no bundle of memories—then is it silence? Is it something intermittent which comes and goes according to your body chemistry? Does it come when you are alone, or with people, or when you are trying to meditate? What we are trying to find out is the nature of this silence. Is it rich or poor? I don't mean rich with experience, or poor because it is uneducated. Is it full or shallow? Is it innocent or is it put together? A mind can look at a fact and not see the beauty, the depth, the quality of that fact. Is it possible to observe silence without the observer? When there is silence, there is only silence, and nothing else. Then in that silence what takes place? Is this what you are asking?

Q: Yes.

K: Is there an observation of silence by silence in silence?

Q: That's a new question.

K: It is not a new question if you have been following. The whole brain, the mind, the feelings, the body, everything is quiet. Can this quietness, stillness, look at itself, not as an observer who is still? Can the totality of this silence watch its own totality? The silence becomes aware of it-self—in this there is no division between an observer and an observed. That is the main point. The silence does not use itself to discover something beyond itself. There is only that silence. Now see what happens.

4

QUESTIONER: I have one predominating habit; I have other habits, but they are of less importance. I have been fighting this one habit as long as I can remember. It must have been formed in early childhood. Nobody seemed to care enough to correct it then and gradually as I grew older it became more and more deep-rooted. It disappears sometimes only to come back again. I don't seem able to get rid of it. I would like to be completely master of it. It has become a mania with me to overcome it. What am I to do?

KRISHNAMURTI: From what you say you have fallen into a habit for many, many years and you have cultivated another habit, the habit of fighting it. So you want to get rid of one habit by cultivating another which is the denial of the first. You are fighting one habit with another. When you can't get rid of the first habit you feel guilty, ashamed, depressed, perhaps angry with yourself for your weakness. The one habit and the other are the two sides of the same

49

coin: without the first, the second wouldn't be, so the second is really a continuation of the first as a reaction. So now you have two problems whereas in the beginning you had only one.

Q: I know what you are going to say because I know what you say about awareness, but I can't be aware all the time.

K: So now you have several things going on at the same time: first of all the original habit, then, the desire to get rid of it, then the frustration of having failed, then the resolve to be aware all the time. This network has arisen because deeply you want to get rid of that one habit; that is your one drive, and you are all the time balancing between the habit and the fighting of it. You don't see that the real problem is having habits, good or bad, not just one particular habit. So the question really is, is it possible to break a habit without any effort, without cultivating its opposite, without suppressing it through uninterrupted vigilance—which is resistance? Uninterrupted vigilance is simply another habit since it is generated by the habit it is trying to overcome.

Q: You mean, can I get rid of the habit without generating this complicated network of reactions to it?

K: So long as you want to get rid of it, that complicated network of reactions is actually in operation. The wanting to get rid of it is that reactionary network. So really you have not stopped this futile reaction to the habit.

Q: But all the same, I must do something about it!

K: That indicates that you are dominated by this one desire. This desire and its reactions are not different from
the habit, and they feed on each other. The desire to be
superior is not different from being inferior, so the superior
is the inferior. The saint is the sinner.

Q: Should I, then, just do nothing about it at all?

K: What you are doing about it is to cultivate another
habit in opposition to the old one.

Q: So if I do nothing, I am left with the habit, and we are
back where we started.

K: Are we though? Knowing that what you do to break
the habit is the cultivation of another habit, there can be
only one action, which is to do nothing at all against that
habit. Whatever you do is in the pattern of habits, so to
do nothing, to have the feeling that you don't have to fight
it, is the greatest action of intelligence. If you do anything
positive you are back in the field of habits. Seeing this very
clearly, there is immediately a feeling of great relief and
great lightness. You now see that fighting one habit by
cultivating another does not end the first habit so you stop
fighting it.

Q: Then only the habit remains, and there is no resistance to it.

K: Any form of resistance feeds the habit, which does not mean that you go on with the habit. You become aware of the habit and of the cultivation of its opposite, which is also a habit, and this awareness shows you that whatever you do with regard to the habit is the formation of another habit. So now, after having observed this whole process, your intelligence says, don't do anything about the habit. Don't give any attention to it. Don't be concerned with it because the more you are concerned with it the more active it becomes. Now intelligence is in operation and is watching. This watching is entirely different from the vigilance of resisting the habit, reacting to it. If you get the feeling of this intelligence watching, then this feeling will operate and deal with the habit, and not the vigilance of resolution and will. So what is important is not habit but the understanding of habit, which brings about intelligence. This intelligence keeps awake without the fuel of desire, which is will. In the first instance the habit is confronted with resistance; in the second it is not confronted at all, and that is intelligence. The action of intelligence has withered the resistance to the habit on which the habit feeds.

Q: Do you mean to say that I have got rid of my habit?

K: Go slowly. Don't be too hasty in your assumption of having got rid of it. What is more important than habit is this understanding, which is intelligence. This intelligence is sacred and therefore must be touched with clean hands, not exploited for trivial little games. Your little habit is utterly unimportant. If intelligence is there, the habit is trivial. If intelligence is not there, then the wheel of habit is all you have got.

5

QUESTIONER: I find I get dreadfully attached to people and dependent on them. In my relationships this attachment develops into a sort of possessive demand which brings about a feeling of domination. Being dependent, and seeing the discomfort and pain of it, I try to be detached. Then I feel terribly lonely, and unable to face the loneliness, I escape from it through drink and in other ways. Yet I don't want to have merely superficial and casual relationships.

KRISHNAMURTI: There is attachment, then the struggle to be detached, then out of this comes deeper conflict, the fear of loneliness. So what is your problem, what is it you are trying to find out, to learn? Whether all relationship is a matter of dependence? You are dependent on environment and people. Is it possible to be free, not only of environment and people, but to be free in yourself, so that you don't depend on anything or anyone? Can there be joy that is not the outcome of environment or of people? The environment changes, people change, and if you depend on them you are caught by them, or else you become indifferent, callous, cynical, hard. So is it not a matter of whether you can live a life of freedom and joy that is not the result of environment, human or otherwise? This is a very important question. Most human beings are slaves to their family or to their circumstances, and they want to change the circumstances and the people, hoping thereby to find joy, to live freely and more openly. But even if they do create their own environment or choose their own relationships, they soon come to depend again on the new environment and the new friends. Does dependence in any form bring joy? This dependence is also the urge to express, the urge to be something. The man who has a certain gift or capacity depends on it, and when it diminishes or goes altogether he is at a loss and becomes miserable and ugly. So to depend psychologically on anything—people, possessions, ideas, talent—is to invite sorrow. Therefore one asks: Is there a joy that is not dependent on anything? Is there a light that is not lit by another?

Q: My joy so far has always been lit by something or someone external to myself, so I can't answer that question. Perhaps I don't even dare to ask it because then I may have to change my way of life. I certainly depend on drink, books, sex, and companionship.

K: But when you see for yourself, clearly, that this dependence breeds various forms of fear and misery, don't you inevitably ask the other question, which is not how to be free of environment and people but, rather, whether there is a joy, a bliss, that is its own light?

Q: I may ask it but it has no value. Being caught in all this, this is all that actually exists for me.

K: What you are concerned with is dependence, with all its implications, which is a fact. Then there is a deeper fact, which is loneliness, the feeling of being isolated. Feeling lonely, we attach ourselves to people, drink, and all sorts of other escapes. Attachment is an escape from loneliness. Can this loneliness be understood and can one find out for oneself what is beyond it? That is the real question, not what to do about attachment to people or environment. Can this deep sense of loneliness, emptiness, be transcended? Any movement at all away from loneliness strengthens the loneliness, and so there is more need than ever before to get away from it. This makes for attachment which brings its own problems. The problems of attachment occupy the mind so much that one loses sight of the loneliness and disregards it. So we disregard the cause and occupy ourselves with the effect. But the loneliness is acting all the time because there is no difference between cause and effect. There is only what is. It becomes a cause only when it moves away from itself. It is important to understand that this movement away from itself is itself, and therefore it is its own effect. There is, therefore, no cause and effect at all, no movement anywhere at all, but only what is. You don't see what is because you cling to the effect. There is loneliness, and apparent movement

56

away from this loneliness to attachment; then this attachment with all its complications becomes so important, so dominating, that it prevents one from looking at what is. Movement away from what is, is fear, and we try to resolve it by another escape. This is perpetual motion, apparently away from what is, but in actuality there is no movement at all. So it is only the mind which sees what is and doesn't move away from it in any direction that is free of what is. Since this chain of cause and effect is the action of loneliness, it is clear that the only ending of loneliness is the ending of this action.

Q: I shall have to go into this very, very deeply.

K: But this also can become an occupation which becomes an escape. If you see all this with complete clarity it is like the flight of the eagle that leaves no mark in the air.

6

QUESTIONER: I have come to you to find out why there is a division, a separation, between oneself and everything else, even between one's wife and children and oneself. Wherever one goes, one finds this separation, not only in oneself but in everyone else. People talk a great deal about unity and brotherhood but I wonder if it is ever possible to be really free of this division, this aching separation? I can pretend, intellectually, that there is no real separation; I can explain to myself the causes of these divisions—not only between man and man but between theories, theologies, and governments—but I know, actually in myself, that there is this insoluble division, this wide gulf that separates me from another. I always feel I'm standing on this bank and that everybody else is on the other bank, and there are these deep waters between us. That's my problem—why is there this gap of separation?

KRISHNAMURTI: You have forgotten to mention the difference, the contradiction, the gap, between one thought and another, between one feeling and another, the contradiction between actions, the division between life and death, the endless corridor of opposites. After stating all this, our question is: why is there this division, this cleavage between what is and what has been or what should be? We are asking why man has lived in this dualistic state, why he has broken life into various fragments. Are we asking to find the cause or are we trying to go beyond the cause and the effect? Is it an analytical process or a perception, an understanding of a state of mind in which division no longer exists? To understand such a state of mind we must look at the beginning of thought. We must be aware of thought as it arises and must also be aware of that which it comes out of. Thought arises from the past. The past is thought. When we say we must be aware of thought as it arises, we mean we must be aware of the actual meaning of thought, not simply the fact that thinking is taking place. It is the meaning of thought which is the past. There is no thought without its meaning. A thought is like a thread in a piece of cloth. Most of us are unaware of the whole cloth, which is the whole mind, and are trying to control, or shape, or understand, the meaning of one thread, which is a thought. On what is the whole cloth of thoughts resting? Is it lying on any substance? If so, what is that substance? Is it lying on deeper thought or on nothing at all? And what is the material of this cloth?

Q: You are asking too many questions. None of this has ever occurred to me before, so I must go rather slowly.

K: Is thought the cause of all division, of all fragmentation in life? What is thought made of? What is the substance

59

of those pieces of thread woven into that complex cloth we call the mind? Thought is matter, probably measurable. And it comes from the accumulated memory, which is matter, stored in the brain. Thought has its origin in the past, recent or remote. Can one be aware of thought as it arises out of the past—the recollections of the past, the action of the past? And can one be aware beyond the past, behind the wall of the past? This doesn't mean still further back in time, it means the space that is not touched by time or memory. Until we discover this, the mind cannot see itself in terms of anything other than thought, which is time. You cannot look at thought with thought, and you cannot look at time with time. So whatever thought does, or whatever it negates, is still within its own measurable boundaries.

To answer all the questions we have put, we must put yet a further question: what is the thinker? Is the thinker separate from thought? Is the experiencer different from the thing he experiences? Is the observer different from the thing he observes? If the observer is different from the thing he observes, then there will always be division, separation, and therefore conflict. To go beyond this cleavage we must understand what the observer is. Obviously he makes this division. You who are observing make this division, whether it be between you and your wife, or the tree, or anything else. Now what is this observer, or thinker, or experiencer? The observer is the living entity who is always moving, acting, who is aware of things, and aware of his own existence. This existence he is aware of is his relationship to things, to people, and to ideas.

This observer is the whole machinery of thought, he is also observation, he is also a nervous system and sensory perception. The observer is his name, his conditioning, and the relationship between that conditioning and life. All this is the observer. He is also his own idea of himself—an image again built from conditioning, from the past, from tradition. The observer thinks and acts. His action is always according to his image about himself and his image of the world. This action of the observer in relationship breeds division. This action is the only relationship we know. This action is not separate from the observer, it is the observer himself. It is the observer who talks about the world and himself in relationship, and fails to see that his relationship is his own action, therefore himself. So the cause of all the division is the action of the observer. The observer himself is the action which divides life into the thing observed and himself separate from it. Here is the basic cause of division, and hence conflict.

The division in our lives is the structure of thought, which is the action of the observer who thinks himself separate. He further thinks of himself as the thinker, as something different from his thought. But there can be no thought without the thinker and no thinker without the thought. So the two are really one. He is also the experiencer and, again, he separates himself from the thing he experiences. The observer, the thinker, the experiencer, are not different from the observed, the thought, the experienced. This is not a verbal conclusion. If it is a conclusion then it is another thought which again makes the division between the conclusion and the action which is supposed to follow that conclusion. When the mind sees the reality of this, the division can no longer exist. This is the whole point of what we are saying. All conflict is this battle between the observer and the observed. This is the greatest thing to understand. Only now can we answer our questions; only now can we go beyond the wall of time and memory, which is thought, because only now has thought come to an end. It is only now that thought cannot breed division. Thought which can function to communicate, to act, to work, is another kind of thought which does not breed division in relationship. Righteousness is living without the separative action of the observer.

Q: What then, where then, is that thing on which the cloth of thought exists?

K: It is that which is not the action of the observer. The realizing of this is great love. This realization is possible only when you understand that the observer himself is the observed—and that is meditation.

7

QUESTIONER: I am in conflict over so many things, not only outwardly but also inwardly. I can somehow deal with the outward conflicts but I want to know how I can end the conflict, the battle, which is going on within myself most of the time. I want to be finished with it. I want somehow to be free from all this strife. What am I to do? Sometimes it seems to me that conflict is inevitable. I see it in the struggle for survival, the big living on the little, the great intellect dominating smaller intellects, one belief suppressing, supplanting another, one nation ruling another, and so on, endlessly. I see this and accept it, but it doesn't somehow seem right; it doesn't seem to have any quality of love, and I feel that if I could end this strife in myself, out of that ending might come love. But I'm so uncertain, so confused, about the whole thing. All the great teachers have maintained that one must strive, that the way to find truth, or God, is through discipline, control, and sacrifice. In one form or another this battle is sanctified. And now you say that conflict is the very root of disorder. How am I to know what is the truth about conflict?

KRISHNAMURTI: Conflict in any form distorts the mind. This is a fact, not some opinion or judgment given thoughtlessly. Any conflict between two people prevents their understanding each other. Conflict prevents perception. The understanding of what is is the only important thing, not the formulating of what should be. This division between what is and what should be is the origin of conflict. And the interval between idea and action also breeds conflict. The fact and the image are two different things. The pursuit of the image leads to every form of conflict, illusion, and hypocrisy, whereas the understanding of what is, which is the only thing we really have, leads to quite a different state of mind.

Contradictory drives bring about conflict; one will opposing another form of desire is conflict. Memory of what has been, opposed to what is, is conflict; and this is time. Becoming, achieving, is conflict, and this is time. Imitation, conformity, obedience, taking a vow, regretting, suppressing—all this brings more or less conflict. The very structure of the brain, which demands security, safety, which is aware of danger, is the source of conflict. There is no such thing as security or permanency. So our whole being, our relationships, activities, thoughts, our way of life, engender struggle, conflict, strife. And now you ask me how this is to end. The saint, the monk, and the sannyasi try to escape from conflict, but they are still in conflict. As we know, all relationship is conflict—conflict between the image and the reality. There is no relation-ship between two people, not even between the two im-ages they have of each other. Each lives in his own isolation, and the relationship is merely looking over the wall. So wherever one looks, superficially or very, very deeply, there is this agony of strife and pain. The whole field of the mind, in its aspirations, in its desire to change, in its acceptance of what is and its wanting to go beyond it, is itself conflict. So the mind itself is conflict, thought is conflict, and when thought says, "I will not think," this also is conflict. All activity of the mind and of the feelings, which are part of the mind, is conflict. When you ask how you can end conflict you are really asking how you can stop thinking, how your mind can be drugged to be quiet.

Q: But I don't want a drugged, stupid mind. I want it to be highly active, energetic, and passionate. Must it be either drugged or in conflict?

K: You want it to be active, energetic, passionate, and yet you want to end conflict?

Q: Precisely, for when there is conflict it is neither active nor passionate. When there is conflict, it is as if the mind were wounded by its own activity and loses sensitivity.

K: So it becomes clear that conflict destroys passion, en-ergy, and sensitivity.

Q: You don't have to convince me. I know it, but it doesn't get me any further.

K: What do you mean by knowing?

Q: I mean that the truth of what you have said is apparent, but this gets one no further.

K: Do you see the truth of it, or do you see the verbal structure of it—the actual fact or the explanation? We must be very clear about this because the explanation is not the fact, the description is not the described; and when you say "I know," it may be that you perceive only the description.

Q: No.

K: Please don't be so quick and impatient. If the description is not the described, then there is only the described. The described is the fact, this fact: passion, sensitivity, and energy are lost when there is conflict. And conflict is all thinking and feeling, which is all the mind. The mind is all like and dislike, judgment, prejudice, condemnation, justification, and so on. And one very important activity of the mind is description, in which it gets caught. The mind sees its own description and gets caught in it and thinks it sees the fact, whereas in reality it is caught up in its own movement. So where are we now, when there is only what is and not the description?

Q: You were saying there is conflict, which is all the actions of the mind, and this conflict destroys the sensitivity and the energy and the passion of the mind itself. So the mind dulls itself by conflict, by working against itself.

K: So your question becomes: how can the mind stop working against itself?

Q: Yes.

K: Is this question one more condemnation, justification, escape, one more of these interfering activities of the mind which makes it work against itself? If it is, then it breeds conflict. Is this question trying to get rid of conflict? If it is, it is more conflict, and you are forever in this vicious circle. So the right question is not how to end conflict but to see the truth that where passion and sensitivity are, conflict is absent. Do you see this?

Q: Yes.

K: So you can no longer be concerned with the ending of conflict; it will wither away. But it will never wither so long as thought is nourishing it. What is important is the passion and the sensitivity, not the ending of conflict.

Q: I see this, but that doesn't mean I've got the passion, it doesn't mean I've ended the conflict.

K: If you really see this, that very act of seeing is passion, sensitivity, energy. And in this seeing there is no conflict.

8

QUESTIONER: I left the world, my world of professional writing, because I wanted to lead a spiritual life. I abandoned all my appetites and ambitions to be famous, although I had the necessary talent, and came to you hoping to find, to realize, the ultimate. I have been under this great banyan tree for five years now and I find myself all of a sudden dull, washed out, inwardly lonely, and rather miserable. I wake up in the morning to find that I have not realized anything at all, that I was perhaps better off a couple of years ago when I still had some strong religious fervor. Now there is no fervor left and, having sacrificed the things of the world to find God, I am without either. I feel like a sucked orange. What is to blame? Is it the teachings, you, your environment, or is it that I have no capacity for this thing, that I have not found the crack in the wall that will reveal the sky? Or is it simply that this whole quest, from beginning to end, is a mirage and that I would have been better off never to have thought of religion but to have stuck to the tangible, everyday fulfillments of my former life? What is wrong, and what am I to do now? Shall I leave all this? If so, for what?

KRISHNAMURTI: Do you feel that living under this banyan tree, or any other tree, is destroying you, preventing you from understanding, seeing? Is this environment destroying you? If you leave this world and go back to what you did before—the world of writing and all the everyday things of life—will you not be destroyed, dulled, and sucked dry there also by the things of that life? You see this destructive process going on everywhere in people who pursue success, whatever they are doing and for whatever reason. You see it in the doctor, in the politician, in the scientist, in the artist. Does anyone anywhere ever escape this destruction?

Q: Yes, I see that everyone is sucked dry. They may have fame and wealth, but if they look at themselves objectively they have to admit that they are actually nothing more than a showy facade of actions, words, formulas, concepts, attitudes, platitudes, hopes, and fears. Underneath there is emptiness and confusion, age and the bitterness of failure.

K: Do you also see that the religious people who have supposedly abandoned the world are still really in it because their conduct is governed by the same ambitions, the same drive to fulfill, to become, to realize, to attain, to grasp, and to keep? The objects of this drive are called spiritual and seem to be different from the objects of the drive in the world, but they are not different at all because the

69

drive is exactly the same movement. These religious people also are caught in formulas, ideals, imagination, hopes,
vague certainties, which are only beliefs, and they also
become old, ugly, and hollow. So the world which they
have left is exactly the same as the world of the so-called
spiritual life. In this so-called spiritual world. you are destroyed just as you were destroyed in that other everyday
world.

Do you think that this dying, this destruction, comes
from your environment or from yourself? Does it come
from another or from you? Is it something that is done to
you or something that you are doing?

Q: I thought that this dying, this destruction, was the result of my environment, but now that you have pointed
out how it takes place in all environments everywhere,
and continues even when you change the environment, I
am beginning to see that this destruction is not the result
of environment. This dying is self-destruction. It is something which I do to myself. It is I who do it, I who am
responsible, and it has nothing to do with people or environment.

K: This is the most important point to realize. This destruction comes from yourself and from nobody and nothing else, not from your environment, not from people, not
from events or circumstances. You are responsible for your
own destruction and misery, your own loneliness, your
own moods, your own empty hollowness. When you realize this you either become bitter or insensitive to it all,

pretending that all is well; or you become neurotic, vacillating between one world and the other, thinking that there is some difference between them, or you take to drink or drugs like so many people have done.

Q: I understand this now.

K: In that case you will abandon all hope of finding a solution by simply changing the outer environment of your life, by simply changing from one world to the other, for you will know that both are the same; in both of them is the desire to achieve, to attain, to gain the ultimate pleasure, whether in so-called enlightenment, God, truth, love, a fat bank account, or any other form of security.

Q: I see this, but what am I to do? I am still dying, still destroying myself. I feel sucked dry, empty, useless. I have lost all I had and gained nothing in return.

K: You have not understood then when you feel and say that, you are still walking the same road we have been talking about, that road of self-fulfillment in either world. That road is the self-killing, that road is the factor of dying. Your feeling that you have lost all and gained nothing in return is to walk that road; that road is the destruction; the road itself is its own destruction which is self-destruction, frustration, loneliness, immaturity. So the question now is, have you really turned your back on that road?

71

Q: How do I know whether I have turned my back on it or not?

K: You don't know, but if you see what that road actually is, not only its end but its beginning, which is the same as its end, then it is impossible for you to walk on it. You may, knowing the danger of it, occasionally stray on to it in a moment of inattention and then catch yourself on it suddenly, but seeing the road and its desolation is the ending of that road, and this is the only act. Don't say, "I don't understand it, I must think about it, I must work at it, I must practice awareness, I must find out what it is to be attentive, I must meditate and go into it," but see that every movement of fulfillment, achievement, or dependence in life is that road. Seeing this is the abandonment of that road. When you see danger you don't make a great fuss trying to make up your mind what to do about it. If, in the face of danger, you say, "I must meditate about it, become aware of it, go into it, understand it," you are lost, it is too late. So what you have to do is simply to see this road, what it is, where it leads and how it feels—and already you will be walking in a different direction.

This is what we mean when we speak of awareness. We mean to be aware of the road and all the significance of that road, to be aware of the thousand different movements in life which are on the same road. If you try to see or walk on the "other" road, you are still on the same old road.

Q: How can I be sure that I am seeing what to do?

K: You can't see what to do, you can see only what not to do. The total negation of that road is the new beginning, the other road. This other road is not on the map, nor can it ever be put on any map. Every map is a map of the wrong road, the old road.

MEDITATIONS
1969

1

IN THE SPACE which thought creates around itself there is no love. This space divides man from man, and in it is all the becoming, the battle of life, the agony and fear. Meditation is the ending of this space, the ending of the me. Then relationship has quite a different meaning, for in that space which is not made by thought, the other does not exist, for you do not exist. Meditation then is not the pursuit of some vision, however sanctified by tradition. Rather it is the endless space where thought cannot enter. To us, the little space made by thought around itself, which is the me, is extremely important, for this is all the mind knows, identifying itself with everything that is in that space. And the fear of not being is born in that space. But in meditation, when this is understood, the mind can enter into a dimension of space where action is inaction. We do not know what love is, for in the space made by thought around itself as the me, love is the conflict of the me and the not-me. This conflict, this torture, is not love.

Thought is the very denial of love, and it cannot enter into that space where the me is not. In that space is the benediction which man seeks and cannot find. He seeks it within the frontiers of thought, and thought destroys the ecstasy of this benediction.

2

PERCEPTION without the word, which is without thought, is one of the strangest phenomena. Then the perception is much more acute, not only with the brain, but also with all the senses. Such perception is not the fragmentary perception of the intellect nor the affair of the emotions. It can be called a total perception, and it is part of meditation. Perception without the perceiver in meditation is to commune with the height and depth of the immense. This perception is entirely different from seeing an object without an observer, because in the perception of meditation there is no object and therefore no experience. Meditation can, however, take place when the eyes are open and one is surrounded by objects of every kind. But then these objects have no importance at all. One sees them but there is no process of recognition, which means there is no experiencing.

What meaning has such meditation? There is no meaning; there is no utility. But in that meditation there is a movement of great ecstasy which is not to be confounded with pleasure. It is this ecstasy which gives to the eye, to the brain, and to the heart, the quality of innocency. Without seeing life as something totally new, it is a routine, a boredom, a meaningless affair. So meditation is of the greatest importance. It opens the door to the incalculable, to the measureless.

3

WHEN YOU TURN your head from horizon to horizon, your eyes see a vast space in which all the things of the earth and of the sky appear. But this space is always limited where the earth meets the sky. The space in the mind is so small. In this little space all our activities seem to take place, the daily living and the hidden struggles with contradictory desires and motives. In this little space the mind seeks freedom, and so it is always a prisoner of itself. Meditation is the ending of this little space. To us, action is bringing about order in this little space of the mind. But there is another action which is not putting order in this little space. Meditation is action which comes when the mind has lost its little space. This vast space which the mind, the I, cannot reach, is silence. The mind can never be silent within itself; it is silent only within the vast space which thought cannot touch. Out of this silence there is action which is not of thought. Meditation is this silence.

4

MEDITATION is one of the most extraordinary things, and if you do not know what it is you are like the blind man in a world of bright color, shadows, and moving light. It is not an intellectual affair, but when the heart enters into the mind, the mind has quite a different quality; it is really, then, limitless, not only in its capacity to think, to act efficiently, but also in its sense of living in a vast space where you are part of everything. Meditation is the movement of love. It isn't the love of the one or of the many. It is like water that anyone can drink out of any jar, whether golden or earthenware; it is inexhaustible. And a peculiar thing takes place which no drug or self-hypnosis can bring about: it is as though the mind enters into itself, beginning at the surface and penetrating ever more deeply, until depth and height have lost their meaning and every form of measurement ceases. In this state there is complete peace—not contentment that has come about through gratification—but a peace that has order, beauty, and intensity. It can all be destroyed, as you can destroy a flower, and yet because of its very vulnerability it is indestructible.

This meditation cannot be learned from another. You must begin without knowing anything about it, and move from innocence to innocence.

The soil in which the meditative mind can begin is the soil of everyday life, the strife, the pain, and the fleeting joy. It must begin there, and bring order, and from there move endlessly. But if you are concerned only with making order, then that very order will bring about its own limitation, and the mind will be its prisoner. In all this movement you must somehow begin from the other end, from the other shore, and not always be concerned with this shore or how to cross the river. You must take a plunge into the water not knowing how to swim. And the beauty of meditation is that you never know where you are, where you are going, what the end is.

5

Is THERE a new experience in meditation? The desire for experience, the higher experience which is beyond and above the daily or the commonplace, is what keeps the well-spring empty. The craving for more experience, for visions, for higher perception, for some realization or other, makes the mind look outward, which is no different from its dependence on environment and people. The curious part of meditation is that an event is not made into an experience. It is there, like a new star in the heavens, without memory taking it over and holding it, without the habitual process of recognition and response in terms of like and dislike. Our search is always outgoing; the mind seeking any experience is outgoing. Inward-going is not a search at all; it is perceiving. Response is always repetitive, for it comes always from the same bank of memory.

6

AFTER THE RAINS the hills were splendid. They were still brown from the summer sun, and soon all the green things would come out. It had rained quite heavily, and the beauty of those hills was indescribable. The sky was still clouded and in the air there was the smell of sumac, sage, and eucalyptus. It was splendid to be among them, and a strange stillness possessed you. Unlike the sea which lay far down below you, those hills were completely still. As you watched and looked about you, you had left everything down below in that little house—your clothes, your thoughts, and the odd ways of life. Here you were traveling very lightly, without any thoughts, without any burden, and with a feeling of complete emptiness and beauty. The little green bushes would soon be still greener, and in a few weeks' time they would have a stronger smell. The quails were calling and a few of them flew over. Without knowing it, the mind was in a state of meditation in which love was flowering. After all, only in the soil of meditation can this flower bloom. It was really quite marvelous, and, strangely, all through the night it pursued you, and when you woke, long before the sun was up, it was still there in your heart with its incredible joy, for no reason whatsoever. It was there, causeless, and was quite intoxicating. It would be there all through the day without your ever asking or inviting it to stay with you.

7

IT HAD RAINED heavily during the night and the day, and down the gullies the muddy stream poured into the sea, making it chocolate-brown. As you walked on the beach the waves were enormous, and they were breaking with magnificent curve and force. You walked against the wind, and suddenly you felt there was nothing between you and the sky, and this openness was heaven. To be so completely open, vulnerable—to the hills, to the sea, and to man—is the very essence of meditation.

To have no resistance, to have no barriers inwardly toward anything, to be really free, completely, from all the minor urges, compulsions, and demands, with all their little conflicts and hypocrisies, is to walk in life with open arms. And that evening, walking there on that wet sand, with the seagulls around you, you felt the extraordinary sense of open freedom and the great beauty of love which was not in you or outside you but everywhere.

We don't realize how important it is to be free of the nagging pleasures and their pains, so that the mind remains alone. It is only the mind that is wholly alone that is open. You felt all this suddenly, like a great wind that swept over the land and through you. There you were—denuded of everything, empty—and therefore utterly open. The beauty of it was not in the word or in the feeling, but seemed to be everywhere—about you, inside you, over the waters, and in the hills. Meditation is this.

8

IT WAS ONE of those lovely mornings that have never been before. The sun was just coming up and you saw it between the eucalyptus and the pine. It was over the waters, golden, burnished—such light that exists only between the mountains and the sea. It was such a clear morning, breathless, full of that strange light that one sees not only with one's eyes but with one's heart. And when you see it the heavens are very close to earth, and you are lost in the beauty. You know, you should never meditate in public, or with another, or in a group; you should meditate only in solitude, in the quiet of the night, or in the still, early morning. When you meditate in solitude, it must be solitude. You must be completely alone, not following a system, a method, repeating words, pursuing a thought, or shaping a thought according to your desire.

This solitude comes when the mind is freed from thought. When there are influences of desire or of the things that the mind is pursuing, either in the future or in the past, there is no solitude. Only in the immensity of the present this aloneness comes. And then, in quiet secrecy in which all communication has come to an end, in which there is no observer with his anxieties, with his stupid appetites and problems—only then, in that quiet aloneness, meditation becomes something that cannot be put into words. Then meditation is an eternal movement.

I don't know if you have ever meditated, if you have ever been alone, by yourself, far away from everything, from every person, from every thought and pursuit, if you have ever been completely alone, not isolated, not withdrawn into some fanciful dream or vision, but far away, so that in yourself there is nothing recognizable, nothing that you touch by thought or feeling, so far away that in this full solitude the very silence becomes the only flower, the only light, and the timeless quality that is not measurable by thought. Only in such meditation love has its being. Don't bother to express it; it will express itself. Don't use it. Don't try to put it into action; it will act, and when it acts, in that action there is no regret, no contradiction, none of the misery and travail of man.

So meditate alone. Get lost. And don't try to remember where you have been. If you try to remember it, then it will be something that is dead. And if you hold on to the memory of it, then you will never be alone again. So meditate in that endless solitude, in the beauty of that love, in that innocency, in the new. Then there is the bliss that is imperishable.

The sky is very blue, the blue that comes after the rain, and these rains have come after many months of drought.

After the rain the skies are washed clean and the hills are rejoicing, and the earth is still. And every leaf has the light of the sun on it, and the feeling of the earth is very close to you. So meditate in the very secret recesses of your heart and mind, where you have never been before.

9

THAT MORNING the sea was like a lake or an enormous river, without a ripple and so calm that you could see the reflections of the stars so early in the morning. The dawn had not yet come, and so the stars, and the reflection of the cliff, and the distant lights of the town, were there on the water. And as the sun came up over the horizon in a cloudless sky it made a golden path, and it was extraordinary to see that light of California filling the earth and every leaf and blade of grass. As you watched, a great stillness came into you. The brain itself became very quiet, without any reaction, without a movement, and it was strange to feel this immense stillness. *Feel* isn't the word; the quality of that silence, that stillness, is not felt by the brain; it is beyond the brain. The brain can conceive, formulate, or make a design for the future, but this stillness is beyond its range, beyond all imagination, beyond all desire. You are so still that your body becomes completely part of the earth, part of everything that is still.

And as the slight breeze came from the hills, stirring the leaves, this stillness, this extraordinary quality of silence, was not disturbed. The house was between the hills and the sea, overlooking the sea. And as you watched the sea, so very still, you really became part of everything. You were everything. You were the light, and the beauty of love. Again, to say "you were a part of everything" is also wrong; the word *you* is not adequate, because you really weren't there. You didn't exist. There was only that stillness, the beauty, the extraordinary sense of love. The words *you* and *I* separate things. This division, in this strange silence and stillness, doesn't exist. And as you watched out of the window, space and time seemed to have come to an end, and the space that divides had no reality. That leaf and that eucalyptus and the blue shining water were not different from you.

Meditation is really very simple. We complicate it. We weave a web of ideas around it, what it is and what it is not. But it is none of these things. Because it is so very simple, it escapes us, because our minds are so complicated, so timeworn and time-based. And this mind dictates the activity of the heart, and then the trouble begins. But meditation comes naturally, with extraordinary ease, when you walk on the sand or look out of your window or see those marvelous hills burnt by last summer's sun. Why are we such tortured human beings, with tears in our eyes and false laughter on our lips? If you could walk alone among those hills or in the woods or along the long, white, bleached sands, in that solitude you would know what meditation is. The ecstasy of solitude comes when you are not frightened to be alone, no longer belonging to the world or attached to anything. Then, like that dawn that came up this morning, it comes silently, and makes a golden path in the very stillness, which was at the beginning, which is now, and which will be always there.

10

HAPPINESS AND PLEASURE you can buy in any market at a price. But bliss you cannot buy, for yourself or for another. Happiness and pleasure are time-binding. Only in total freedom does bliss exist. Pleasure, like happiness, you can seek and find in many ways. But they come and go. Bliss, that strange sense of joy, has no motive. You cannot possibly seek it. Once it is there, depending on the quality of your mind, it remains—timeless, causeless, and a thing that is not measurable by time. Meditation is not the pursuit of pleasure and the search for happiness. Meditation, on the contrary, is a state of mind in which there is no concept or formula, and therefore total freedom. It is only to such a mind that this bliss comes unsought and uninvited. Once it is there, though you may live in the world with all its noise, pleasure, and brutality, they will not touch that mind. Once it is there, conflict has ceased. But the ending of conflict is not necessarily the total freedom. Meditation is a movement of the mind in this freedom. In this explosion of bliss the eyes are made innocent, and love is then benediction.

11

MEDITATION is not the mere control of body and thought, nor is it a system of breathing in and breathing out. The body must be still, healthy, and without strain. Sensitivity of feeling must be sharpened and sustained, and the mind, with all its chattering, disturbances, and gropings, must come to an end. It is not the organism that one must begin with, but rather it is the mind, with its opinions, prejudices, and self-interest, that must be seen to. When the mind is healthy, vital, and vigorous, then feeling will be heightened and will be extremely sensitive. Then the body, with its own natural intelligence which hasn't been spoiled by habit and taste, will function as it should.

So one must begin with the mind and not with the body, the mind being thought and the varieties of expressions of thought. Mere concentration makes thought narrow, limited, and brittle, but concentration comes as a natural thing when there is an awareness of the ways of thought. This awareness does not come from the thinker who chooses and discards, who holds onto and rejects. This awareness is without choice and is both the outer and the inner; it is an interflow between the two, so the division between the outer and the inner comes to an end.

Thought destroys feeling, feeling being love. Thought can offer only pleasure, and in the pursuit of pleasure, love is pushed aside. The pleasure of eating, of drinking, has its continuity in thought, and merely to control or suppress this pleasure, which thought has brought about, has no meaning; it creates only various forms of conflict and compulsion.

Thought, which is matter, cannot seek that which is beyond time, for thought is memory, and the experience in that memory is as dead as the leaf of last autumn.

In awareness of all this comes attention, which is not the product of inattention. It is inattention which has dictated the pleasureable habits of the body and diluted the intensity of feeling. Inattention cannot be made into attention. The awareness of inattention is attention.

The seeing of this whole complex process is meditation, from which alone comes order in this confusion. This order is as absolute as is the order in mathematics, and from this there is action, the immediate doing. Order is not arrangement, design, and proportion; these come much later. Order comes out of a mind that is not cluttered up by the things of thought. When thought is silent there is emptiness, which is order.

INWARD
FLOWERING

DIALOGUE WITH
STUDENTS AND STAFF AT
BROCKWOOD PARK

KRISHNAMURTI: I think it would be good if we could talk over together this morning the question of whether here, in this community, each one of us is flowering, growing, blooming. Or are we following a certain narrow groove, and will therefore realize at the end of life that we have never had an opportunity to flower deeply?

We should ask, I think, as students at Brockwood, not only whether we are now growing physically taller or more strong, but also whether anything is hindering us, blocking or preventing us from deeply growing, flowering, inwardly. Most of us hardly ever flower. Something happens in the course of our lives that stultifies us, that deadens us; there is no deep inward nourishment. Perhaps it is because the world around us demands that we become specialists— doctors, scientists, archaeologists, philosophers, and so on. That may perhaps be one of the reasons why, psychologically, we don't seem to grow immensely. I think this is one of the questions that we, a small community of teachers and students, should discuss here together—whether anything is preventing us from flowering. Are we too deeply conditioned by our society, by our parents, by our religion, by our knowledge even? Are all those environmental influences really preventing, or blocking, or hindering this blossoming? Do you understand my question? You don't understand?

Look, if I am a Catholic, my mind, my brain, my whole psychological structure, is already conditioned, isn't it? My parents tell me I am a Catholic, I go to church every Sunday and there is the Mass, all the beauty of it, the incense, the people to watch and the intoning of the priest. All that conditions the mind, and therefore there is never a flowering. You understand? I move along in a certain groove, a certain path, follow a certain system, and that very path, that very system, that very activity is limiting, and therefore there is never a blossoming. Is that what is happening here?

Are we so heavily conditioned by the many accidents and incidents, and by pressures and assertions of parents that it prevents us from growing easily, happily? If it is that, then does living here at Brockwood help us to break down our conditioning? If it does not, then what's the point of it? What's the point of Brockwood if we're going to turn out like so many millions of people who have never felt or lived in this vast sense of deepening, flowing, flowering? You understand my question? Do you? Please, this is a dialogue, you know; I am not giving a talk.

STUDENT: Outside, there is too much pressure, you know.

K: Too much pressure. Yes, there is too much pressure. Go into it slowly, inquire into it. If you had no pressure would you do anything? Would you even pay attention now? I am pressing you, you understand? I am not actually pushing you into a corner, but I am pointing out to you, and that may also be a pressure because you don't want to look. You want to have fun in life; you think that you are a special person; you want to do one thing and therefore you neglect everything else. But if you had no pressure at all of any kind, would you be active? Or, would you become more and more lazy, indifferent, and gradually wither away? Though you may have a husband, a wife, children, a house, and a job, inwardly the blossoming would never take place.

So are you receiving the right kind of pressure? Not compulsive pressure, not the pressure to imitate, not the pressure of success, climbing the ladder, becoming somebody, but the pressure that helps you to grow inwardly. If there is no flowering, one lives an ordinary mundane life and dies at the end of fifty, sixty, or eighty years. That is the usual life of the average person. When you observe all that, what is your reaction? What do you say about it?

S: One asks if it is meaningful to live that way.

K: No. Look, old boy, you know, as they grow older very few people are happy; there is too much pressure, there is competition, a thousand people for one job, and over-population. Everything in the world is becoming more and

more dangerous. You understand? When you observe all
this, what is your response to it?

S: I can see my parents getting older, I see more of their
insecurities and how they are just running around without
any meaning to their lives.

K: So you are saying that most people in the world are
seeking security, physical security and, perhaps, psychological security. But will security, biological as well as psychological, give you this sense of flowering? I am using the
word *flowering* in the sense of growing—like a flower that
grows in a field without any hindrance. Now, are you seeking both kinds of security, depending psychologically, inwardly on somebody, or on a belief, and identifying with
a nation, with a group? Or are you learning a specific tech-
nological subject so that it will give you outward security
also? Are you seeking both kinds of security in some kind
of knowledge?

You have to ask all these questions to find out, haven't
you? Is there such a thing as psychological security? Do
you understand my question? I depend on my husband, or
wife, for many, many reasons—comfort, sex, encourage-
ment; when I feel lonely or depressed, there is somebody
who says, "It's all right, you're doing very well, how nice
you are," and pats me on the back and that makes me feel
more comfortable, so eventually I become attached and
depend on her or him. Is there security in that relationship? Please discuss it with me.

S: The relationship is very fragile.

K: It is very fragile, but is there permanent security in any relationship at all? You will fall in love—whatever that may mean—and for a few years you will be attached to someone, you will depend on each other in every way. And in that relationship you are seeking the continuity of that feeling all the time, aren't you? But before you completely tie yourself in that knot, which is called "falling in love," mustn't you inquire whether there is any security in any relationship between human beings? Which doesn't mean a hopeless, depressing loneliness.

Because you are lonely, uncomfortable by yourself, insufficient in yourself, afraid that you cannot live alone, you gradually begin to attach yourself because you are frightened. And so what happens? When you are attached, you are equally frightened that you may lose what you are attached to. That person may run away from you, may fall in love with somebody else. So I think it is very important to ask whether there is any security in relationship. If you find there is no security in relationship then you will have to ask if there is security in love. You understand? No, you haven't understood. All right, we will go at it.

I am attached to you, I like you, I "fall in love" with you, I want to marry, have sex, children, and all the rest of it. But is this attachment permanent, lasting? Or is it very fragile, very shaky, uncertain? I want to make it certain, yet in reality it is very uncertain. Right? Yet we say that in relationship there is love. Now is there security in love? And what do we mean by love? Are we going along together in this?

My first question is: is it possible to bloom, to flower, to grow, to be completely over the hills and dancing? Or is life always depressing, lonely, miserable, violent, stupid? You follow? That is the first thing one wants to find out. And is Brockwood helping one to bloom?

In Brockwood there is relationship with each other; you can't help it; you see each other every day. And in this relationship you might fall in love with somebody. Yes? And you get attached to that person. When you are attached you want that attachment to continue, don't you? To last endlessly. You want to find out if there is anything permanent in that relationship. Is that relationship permanent?

You say it is not permanent. How do you know it is not permanent? You may get married, but in that relationship is there a continuity without any conflict, without any quarrels, without isolation, dependence? You say there isn't. But why do you say that? I want to find out why you say it. Will you say it in the first year after you fall in love and get married? Will you? Or only after five years or a dozen years, will you say, "Oh my God, there's no security at all in this"?

And also you have to find out, in this relationship of insecurity, of uncertainty—with the fear, the boredom, the habits, the repetition, seeing the same face over and over again for twenty, thirty, fifty years—whether you will blossom. Will you grow? Will you become a most extraordinarily beautiful, total entity? You also have to find out, when you are in so-called love—which is a much used expression, spoiled, degraded—whether you will blossom.

S: First of all, perhaps the relationship will be much more a relationship between two images.

K: Are you saying that we have images of the man and the woman, and we want those images, or pictures, or conclusions to continue permanently?

S: There is so much of the superficial involved in that relationship that there is no time for investigation into what is real.

K: Listen! What we are talking about first of all is whether you see it as important that one must flower—the importance of it, the truth of it, the reality of it, the necessity of it, the beauty of it—that one must flower. Does relationship, as it is now between two human beings, help you to flower? That is one point. Wait, wait. And we also say we love each other. Will that love nourish the flowering of a human mind, a human heart, of human qualities?

We are also asking, does being here at Brockwood help you to grow, to flourish, not only technologically— becoming a specialist in this or that—but also inwardly, psychologically, under the skin, inside you, so that nothing blocks you, hinders you, so that you are not neurotic or lopsided, but are a whole complete human being, growing, flowering?

So, now we have to ask, what is love? What do you

think it is? You love your parents, and your parents love you. At least, they say so, and you say so. Are we on dangerous ground? Are we? My question is, do they? Don't reply. If they love you, they will see to it that from the moment you are born you are unconditioned, that you flower, because you are a human being. If you do not flower, you are caught in the world, you are destroying other human beings. If your parents love you, they will see that you are properly educated, not only technologically to get a job, but inwardly so that you have no conflict and are not killed in wars. All this is implied when I love my daughter or my son. I don't want my son to be educated and shot to pieces in twenty years' time and have a marble slab or a cross put up in a rotten field. And I don't want him to become just a first-class businessman, getting a lot of money. Or to become a marvelous specialist who may help outwardly a little bit here and there—building better bridges, becoming a better doctor, doing better medicine. What for?

So what is love? What do you think it is? Come on! Isn't it very important for you to find out? Please. Don't you want to find out when you have observed people around you, parents, grandparents, friends, all the world around you? They all use the word *love*, and yet they quarrel, there is competition, they are willing to destroy each other. Is that love? What is love to you then?

S: It is difficult to talk about because you always hear it used in that way.

K: What do *you* feel? Talk about it. What is love to you? I am sure you use the word *love* a great deal, don't you? What does it mean? You know the word *hate*, the meaning of that word. And you know the feeling of it, don't you? Antagonism, anger, jealousy—all that is part of hate isn't it? Even competition is part of hate. Right? So you know the feeling of what it means to hate people, and you can put it down in words very well. Now, is love the opposite of that?

S: The feelings are opposite.

K: I know. Therefore, can you have both in your mind, in your heart, hate and love?

S: We never use them.

K: Stick to it! Do you have such feelings, hate and love, together? Or is one kept in one corner and the other in another corner: "I hate somebody, and I love somebody"? But if you have love, can you hate anybody? Can you kill something, kill people, throw bombs, and do all the rest of what is happening in the world?

So let us go back to the first question: do we feel, both the educator and the one who is being educated here, the great importance of the necessity to grow, flower, mature, not merely physically, but deeply, inwardly? If you don't, then what is the point of it all? What is the point of your being educated? Passing an exam and getting a degree, getting a job, if you're lucky, and setting up house—will all that help you, help a human being, or help each other to blossom? Do come on!

If you were my daughter or my son, that is the first thing I would talk to you about. I would say, look, look around you, at your friends in the school, at the neighbors, see what is happening around you, not according to what you like or don't like; just look at the fact, see exactly what is happening, without any distortion. People who are married are unhappy, have endless quarrels, you know all that goes on. A boy and a girl also have their problems, their troubles. And see the division of people, races, groups—the religious groups, the scientific groups, the business groups, the artistic groups—everything around you is broken up. Do you see that? And who has broken it up? Human beings have done this. That is, thought has done it. Thought says, "I am a Catholic," "I am a Jew," "I am an Arab"; thought says, "I am a Buddhist," "I am a Muslim," "I am a Christian." Thought has created this. So thought, in its very nature, in its very action, must bring about fragmentation, not only in yourself, but outwardly. Do you see that? Or is this too difficult?

S: Sir, you can actually see it; yes, you can see it.

K: Ah, no. I am asking each person. Do you actually see the fact—please listen very carefully—that thought, in its very nature and action, must bring about fragmentation? Do you see the fact? Or do you see the idea? Which is it? Is it an idea or is it a fact?

110

S: It's an idea.

K: It's an idea, isn't it? Why do you make an idea of it? You understand my question? I say, look around you at the wars, the terrors, the bombs, the violence, the competitive society, and in every house constant disturbances in relationships. Do you see it all as a fact, as reality, or is it an abstraction which is called an idea? If it is an idea, why do you make it into an idea?

S: Can we look at the question of whether thought is fragmentary? What do you think is the conditioning? It is not the thought itself, that is just mechanical.

K: No, just listen. Why is thought fragmentary? Why is it broken up in itself? Not its result, why is thought *in itself* limited?

S: That is probably the structure of how it works. It's taking something from the past and comparing it with other things.

K: Isn't thought the result of time? Be sure, don't agree, just observe it, find out! Isn't thought the result of the movement of time? That is, thought is memory, the response of memory. Do you see that? Aren't memory, experience, knowledge, all in the past, modified in the present, and going on? So all that is a movement of time, isn't it? And because it is of the past it must be fragmentary. Thought can never be the whole.

111

Look, I have learned English; it has taken me a few years to learn it and store it up in the brain—the words, the syntax, how to put sentences together. All that took time, didn't it? And any thought springing from that period of time is limited, isn't it? So thought is not whole, complete. Thought can never be complete because it is always limited. Please see this, not as an idea but as an actuality. We said thought is the response of memory. Memory is stored up in the brain through experience and through the constant accumulation of knowledge. And when you are asked something, memory responds. Right? So thought must be limited, because memory is limited, knowledge is limited, time is limited. Do you see this?

Thought has created the problems in the world. You are Dutch, I am German, you are British, he is Chinese. Thought has created this division. Thought has created the religions: thought says, "Jesus is the greatest savior"; go to India and they say, "We have our God who is much better than yours." Thought has created their god, as thought has created the Christians'. So thought has created the wars and the instruments of war. Thought is responsible for all this. Right?

S: All these ideas, of which you have given examples. . . .

K: It is not an idea, it is a fact.

S: Yes, yes, but go on.

K: Not, "Yes, yes, get on with it." I am not going to get on with it. I want to stick to it until you see it. Don't be impatient with me. I'm asking you if you see the fact that you are Indonesian and I am from India. We have different colors, different cultures, but what created the division?

S: The conditioning of the idea, not the thought itself. I know the difference, but I don't care.

K: You may not care, but the people who hate each other care.

S: There is something behind the thought.

K: What is behind the thought? Conditioning. My parents have said to me, "You are a Brahmin, you are a Hindu," and your parents have said, "You are a Christian."

S: There is the instinct to belong to a group.

K: The instinct to belong to a group—why? Because it's much safer to belong to a community?

S: That is the whole trouble.

K: Because you have identified yourself with a small group. Why don't you identify yourself with the total human being, with all the human beings in the world? Why the small group?

I am pointing out that thought has created all these human, psychological, and worldly problems. There is no denying it. Do you see this as a fact, and not as an idea, as

113

much a fact as when you have toothache. You don't say, "It's an idea; I'll think about my toothache!"

Let's put it this way: Is thought love? Can thinking bring about love? Please, we are discussing this, what do you say?

S: If you love somebody, you have to think.

K: No, I am asking you: Can love be cultivated by thought?

S: It's another conditioning.

K: You are not answering. We have said that thought is fragmentary. Right? It will always be fragmentary. The United Nations is fragmentary, put together by thought. Now, I am asking the question: Thought, being fragmented—and in its activity and its action it must bring about fragmentation—then can thought cultivate, bring about love? What do you say?

S: No.

K: When you say "No," be careful, I'm going to trip you on this! When you say, "No," is it again an idea, or is it an actuality? If it is an actuality, then where love is concerned there is no movement of thought. Do you understand this, not understand up here [touching his head] but deeply, inwardly?

S: What do you mean by deeply?

K: Look, be careful. If love is not thought, if it is not based on thought, then what is relationship? If thought is not love, then what is our relationship? What is relationship that is now based on thought? If thought is not love, then what do you do with the actual relationship that you have now?

I say to myself that I see the fact—not the idea, the fact—that thought is not love. But I am married, I have children, I have my wife, my mother; we have images about each other, interacting relationships. Those interacting relationships are the action of images which I have made about my mother, my wife, my children. And this I call "love." Now I am saying that I see that these relationships are based on the image. And also I see very clearly that love is not the product of thought, that love cannot be thought. Then what happens to my relationship with my mother, my wife, my children? Is this too difficult?

S: How do you see this?

K: What do you mean how do I see it? There is no "how"—it isn't a mechanical thing, old boy. Don't you see this actually? Be simple. What are you saying?

S: Well, as you say, love has nothing to do with thought.

K: Love has nothing to do with thought—full stop. Because I see very clearly that thought is a movement in

115

fragmentation. It is a fact, it's an actuality, not an idea. But I am married, I have a wife, I have children. When I realize as an actual fact that my relationships have been based on images, on thought, what takes place? Do some of you understand what I am saying?

S: Are you saying that the love I knew before, I mean the relationship between images which used to be called "love," is different from this?

K: Look, I have been repeating this. I "fell in love," and I am married; I have been married for a number of years and I have children and I have an image about my wife. I have created it, right? She has nagged me, she has bullied me, she has dominated me; or I have dominated her, or I have bullied her. There is this interaction going on, sexually, and so on. I have built a picture about her and she has built a picture about me. That's a fact. That is, this image-building is the movement of thought. Unless you see this, don't move from there! Now, you come along and tell me that thought is a movement of fragmentation. You explain to me very carefully why it is—because it is bound by time, bound by memory, bound by knowledge, and therefore very limited. I see that. And the next step is—when I have seen that, in relationship with my mother, my wife, my children—what am I to do? Have some of you seen this?

What happens when I realize that my relationship with my wife, or girl or boy, or whoever it is, is a movement of time and fragmentation? If you see this, then what is love?

116

Is love the same thing as this? Is love a fragmentation, a picture, an image, a remembrance?

S: At the first feeling of being in love you see something beautiful. Then you would like to crystalize that.

K: Do you see something beautiful? Do you? Don't say yes. Do you actually see something beautiful? When you look at a tree, or a woman, or a man, or a cloud, or a sheet of water, do you see how extraordinarily beautiful it is and remain with that? Do you see it or is it an idea that it is beautiful?

S: At that moment, I do really see it.

K: What takes place at that moment?

S: There is no word.

K: Which means what? No thought, right? So beauty takes place when there is no movement of thought. You agree to this? [Heads nod.] Ah, you agree to this. Why? You are all together in this? How extraordinary! When you see something beautiful, there is the absence of thought. Now, can you stay and not wander away from it, stay in that moment, watching that cloud? There is no thought in operation, so there is no chattering. Thought is totally absent when you see something extraordinarily beautiful.

Watch it carefully, please listen. The cloud, with its light, with its immensity, has taken you over. Right? The

cloud has absorbed you. Which means you, in that absorption, are absent. Do you see this? Next step: a child is
absorbed in a toy. Remove the toy and he is back to his
mischief. That is exactly what has happened. The cloud
has absorbed you, and when the cloud goes away you are
back to yourself. Right?

Now, without being absorbed by a mountain, by a
cloud, by a tree, by the sound of a bird, by the beauty of
the land, can you be totally empty in yourself? Do you
understand? Remove the toy, and the child is back to his
naughtiness, yelling and shouting, but give him another
toy and the toy again takes him over. I'm asking you, without the toy, and therefore with nothing to absorb you, can
there be an absence of yourself? Oh, do answer this; find
out. See the beauty of this.

So beauty is, when you are not. Beauty is, when
thought is absent.

So, love is not thought, is it? Are you beginning to see
the connection? I won't discuss it. If you see the connection, leave it.

I love you, you have absorbed me, I want you, you look
nice, you smell nice, you have nice hair, my glands demand all kinds of things, sex, and so on. I have fallen in
love with you, that is absorption. I cling to you. But my
old self asserts itself in time and says, yes, she was very nice
two years ago, but now I dislike her. I fell in love with her
face, but now look what has happened!

Please see the truth of this: that where there is beauty
there is total absence of thought. So love is the total

absence of "me." Right? Got it? If you have got it you have drunk at the fountain of life.

S: Does the feeling include the being absorbed, or is it just another word?

K: What is feeling? If there is no thought would you have feelings? Look at it carefully. Is beauty feeling? We said beauty is without thought. And is there a feeling when there is no thought? Leave all the rest of it; get the kernel of it, the meat of it, the inside of it, instead of putting all the details together. The details can come later. See the truth of this one thing, which is: where there is beauty, there is no thought. Where there is love there is the absence of "me" who is chattering, chattering with problems, anxiety, fear. When there is the absence of "me," there is love. Right?

S: You look at a cloud, and it goes, and you fall back into yourself.

K: That's right. When you see a cloud, or something beautiful, a bird flying across the sky, your chattering stops, doesn't it, because what you see is much more interesting? When you see a film, you don't think about all your problems, your worries, your fears. You are just absorbed by it, aren't you? Stop the film and you're back to yourself! No?

S: In a way. You begin to see that.

K: Push this much further: ideas are your toys, ideals are your toys, religions are your toys, and they take you over. But the moment these things are questioned, disturbed, you are back to yourself and get frightened.

S: Is there not one thing which is out of it, out of the world of toys?

K: I've shown it to you.

S: Yes, but. . . .

K: Not, yes but! I am going to stick to that. We said— please listen carefully—that thought has created this world. The wars, the businessman, the politician, the artist, the crook—society has made all this. Society is our relationship to each other, which is based on thought. So thought is responsible for this awful mess. Is it so? Or is it an idea? If you say it is an idea, then you are not looking at the actual facts? Right? Now, move from there. Thought, we said, is broken up; whatever it does will break up. Do you see that as an actuality, as something real, as you see me? "Me" is not an idea: I am sitting here. You might like to make an idea of it but the actual fact is I am sitting here.

S: That is all mechanical thought, but is there something behind it which uses it?

K: You have nothing else but mechanical thought. When that mechanical thought stops, then there is something else. But you can't say, "Yes, that is mechanical, let's look into the other." Thought has to stop. And it stops when you see beauty, something like a vast range of mountains with snow-covered peaks. The majesty of it, the grandeur of it takes you over. And when that mountain is not there you are back home with your quarrels, with your thoughts. That's all.

So, I am saying, please find out, sit down, meditate, go into it for yourself: where there is beauty there is total absence of this mischievous thought. And love is like that too.

S: It's all very well, but . . .

K: It's all very well you say, but I've got to go back to my uncle, my aunt, my mother, my grandmother, and to earn money. That's the problem with all of us. So what are you going to do? When you realize, when you see actually that—except technologically and in practical matters—thought is the most mischievous thing, that it is the most deadly thing in relationship, that it destroys love, then what are you going to do? You have to earn money, earn a livelihood; that demands thought, so there you exercise thought. When you have to go to the dentist, you exercise thought. When you have to buy a suit, a dress, you compare; that requires thought. But you realize that thought is deadly in relationship. That's all.

Pax.

A Dialogue with Oneself

I REALIZE that love cannot exist when there is jealousy; love cannot exist when there is attachment. Now, is it possible for me to be free of jealousy and attachment? I realize that I do not love. That is a fact. I am not going to deceive myself; I am not going to pretend to my wife that I love her. I do not know what love is. But I do know that I am jealous and I do know that I am terribly attached to her and that in attachment there is fear, there is jealousy, anxiety; there is a sense of dependence. I do not like to depend but I depend because I am lonely; I am shoved around in the office, in the factory, and I come home and I want to feel comfort and companionship, to escape from myself. Now I ask myself: how am I to be free of this attachment? I am taking that just as an example.

At first, I want to run away from the question. I do not know how it is going to end up with my wife. When I am really detached from her, my relationship to her may change. She might be attached to me and I might not be attached to her or to any other woman. But I am going to investigate. So I will not run away from what I imagine

125

might be the consequence of being totally free of all attachment. I do not know what love is, but I see very
clearly, definitely, without any doubt, that attachment to
my wife means jealousy, possession, fear, anxiety, and I
want freedom from all that. So I begin to inquire; I look
for a method and I get caught in a system. Some guru says,
"I will help you to be detached; do this and this, practice
this and this." I accept what he says because I see the
importance of being free and he promises me that if I do
what he says I will have a reward. But I see that way that I
am looking for a reward. I see how silly I am, wanting to
be free and getting attached to a reward.

I do not want to be attached and yet I find myself getting attached to the idea that somebody, or some book, or
some method, will reward me with freedom from attachment. So, the reward becomes an attachment. So I say,
"Look what I have done; be careful, do not get caught in
that trap." Whether it is a woman, a method, or an idea,
it is still attachment. I am very watchful now for I have
learned something; that is, not to exchange attachment
for something else that is still attachment.

I ask myself, "What am I to do to be free of attachment?" What is my motive in wanting to be free of attachment? Is it not that I want to achieve a state where there
is no attachment, no fear, and so on? And I suddenly realize that motive gives direction and that direction will dic-
tate my freedom. Why have a motive? What is motive? A
motive is a hope, or a desire, to achieve something. I see
that I am attached to a motive. Not only my wife, not
only my idea, the method, but my motive has become my

attachment! So I am all the time functioning within the field of attachment—the wife, the method, and the motive to achieve something in the future. To all this I am attached. I see that it is a tremendously complex thing. I did not realize that to be free of attachment implied all this. Now, I see this as clearly as I see on a map the main roads, the side roads, and the villages. I see it very clearly. Then I say to myself, "Now, is it possible for me to be free of the great attachment I have for my wife, and also of the reward which I think I am going to get, and also of my motive?" To all this I am attached. Why? Is it that I am insufficient in myself? Is it that I am very, very lonely and therefore seek to escape from that feeling of isolation by turning to a woman, an idea, a motive, as if I must hold onto something? I see that it is so, I am lonely and escaping, through attachment to something, from that feeling of extraordinary isolation.

So I am interested in understanding why I am lonely, for I see it is that which makes me attached. That loneliness has forced me to escape through attachment to this or to that and I see that as long as I am lonely the sequence will always be this. What does it mean to be lonely? How does it come about? Is it instinctual, inherited, or is it brought about by my daily activity? If it is an instinct, if it is inherited, it is part of my lot; I am not to blame. But as I do not accept this, I question it and remain with the question. I am watching, and I am not trying to find an intellectual answer. I am not trying to tell the loneliness what it should do, or what it is; I am watching for it to tell me. There is a watchfulness for the loneliness to reveal itself. It will not reveal itself if I run away, if I am frightened, if I resist it. So I watch it. I watch it so that no thought interferes. Watching is much more important than thought coming in. And because my whole energy is concerned with the observation of that loneliness, thought does not come in at all. The mind is being challenged and it must answer. Being challenged, it is in a crisis. In a crisis you have great energy and that energy remains without being interfered with by thought. This is a challenge which must be answered.

I started out having a dialogue with myself. I asked myself what is this strange thing called love; everybody talks about it, writes about it—all the romantic poems, pictures, sex, and all other areas of it. I ask: is there such a thing as love? I see it does not exist when there is jealousy, hatred, fear. So I am not concerned with love anymore; I am concerned with "what is," my fear, my attachment. Why am I attached? I see that one of the reasons—I do not say it is the whole reason—is that I am desperately lonely, isolated. The older I grow the more isolated I become. So I watch it. This is a challenge to find out, and because it is a challenge all energy is there to respond. That is simple. If there is some catastrophe, an accident, or whatever it is, it is a challenge, and I have the energy to meet it. I do not have to ask, "How do I get this energy?" When the house is on fire I have the energy to move, extraordinary energy. I do not sit back and say, "Well, I must get this energy," and then wait; the whole house will be burned by then.

So there is this tremendous energy to answer the question of why there is this loneliness. I have rejected ideas, suppositions, and theories that it is inherited, that it is instinctual. All that means nothing to me. Loneliness is "what is." Why is there this loneliness which every human being, if he is at all aware, goes through, superficially or most profoundly? Why does it come into being? Is it that the mind is doing something which is bringing it about? I have rejected theories about instinct and inheritance and I am asking: is the mind, the brain itself, bringing about this loneliness, this total isolation? Is the movement of thought doing this? Is thought in my daily life creating this sense of isolation? In the office I am isolating myself because I want to become the top executive, therefore thought is working all the time isolating itself. I see that thought is all the time operating to make itself superior; the mind is working itself toward this isolation.

So the problem then is: why does thought do this? Is it the nature of thought to work for itself? Is it the nature of thought to create this isolation? Education brings about this isolation; it gives me a certain career, a certain specialization and so, isolation. Thought, being fragmentary, being limited and time-binding, is creating this isolation. In that limitation it has found security saying, "I have a special career in my life; I am a professor; I am perfectly safe." So my concern is then: why does thought do it? Is it in its very nature to do this? Whatever thought does must be limited.

Now the problem is: can thought realize that whatever it does is limited, fragmented, and therefore isolating, and that whatever it does will be thus? This is a very important point: can thought itself realize its own limitations? Or am

129

I telling it that it is limited? This, I see, is very important to understand; this is the real essence of the matter. If thought realizes itself that it is limited, then there is no resistance, no conflict; it says, "I am that." But if I am telling it that it is limited then I become separate from the limitation. Then I struggle to overcome the limitation; therefore there is conflict and violence, not love.

So does thought realize of itself that it is limited? I have to find out. I am being challenged. Because I am challenged I have great energy. Put differently, does consciousness realize its content is itself? Or is it that I have heard another say, "Consciousness is its content; its content makes up consciousness"? Therefore I say, "Yes, it is so." Do you see the difference between the two? The latter, created by thought, is imposed by the "me." If I impose something on thought, then there is conflict. It is like a tyrannical government imposing on someone; but here that government is what I have created.

So I am asking myself: has thought realized its own limitations? Or is it pretending to be something extraordinary, noble, divine? Which is nonsense, because thought is based on memory. I see that there must be clarity about this point: that there is no outside influence imposing on thought saying it is limited. Then, because there is no imposition, there is no conflict; it simply realizes it is limited; it realizes that whatever it does—its worship of "God," and so on—is limited, shoddy, petty—even though it has created marvelous cathedrals throughout Europe in which to worship.

So there has been in my conversation with myself the

discovery that loneliness is created by thought. Thought has now realized of itself that it is limited and so cannot solve the problem of loneliness. As it cannot solve the problem of loneliness, does loneliness exist? Thought has created this sense of loneliness, this emptiness, because it is limited, fragmentary, divided, and when it realizes this, loneliness is not, and therefore there is freedom from attachment. I have done nothing. I have watched attachment, what is implied in it, greed, fear, loneliness, all that, and by tracing it, observing it, not analyzing it but just looking, looking, and looking, there is the discovery that thought has done all this. Thought, because it is fragmentary, has created this attachment. When it realizes this, attachment ceases. There is no effort made at all. For the moment there is effort, conflict is back again.

In love there is no attachment; if there is attachment there is no love. There has been the removal of the major factor through negation of what it is not, through the negation of attachment. I know what it means in my daily life: no remembrance of anything my wife, my girlfriend, or my neighbor did to hurt me; no attachment to any image thought has created about her—how she has bullied me, how she has given me comfort, how I have had pleasure sexually, all the different things of which the movement of thought has created images. Attachment to those images has gone.

And there are other factors: must I go through all those step by step, one by one? Or is it all over? Must I go through, must I investigate—as I have investigated attachment—fear, pleasure, and the desire for comfort? I see that

I do not have to go through the investigation of all these various factors. I see it at one glance. I have captured it.

So, through negation of what is not love, love is. I do not have to ask what love is. I do not have to run after it. If I run after it, it is not love, it is a reward. So I have negated, I have ended, in that inquiry, slowly, carefully, without distortion, without illusion, everything that it is not—and the other is.

Printed in the United States
by Baker & Taylor Publisher Services